LONDON CAN TAKE IT

A Wartime Blitz and Evacuation Memoir

VALERIE BRAUNSTON

London Can Take It

Published in 2025 by Wrate's Publishing

ISBN 978-1-0686952-4-7

Edited and typeset by Wrate's Editing Services
www.wrateseditingservices.co.uk

CONTENTS

Foreword

Both my mother and father were wartime children who grew up in London and witnessed events that defined their lives. I didn't sit at the dinner table being told to finish my food because of all the starving children in Africa. The reference point in our household was always "during the war..." I was told I was *so* fortunate to live in a household with modern conveniences because they'd had no televisions, no fridges, no cars, no telephones, no central heating, not even sliced bread – the list was endless. I thought they must have lived in caves!

Then there was the hoarding. Nothing of any remote value or use could be thrown out... just in case. Our shed and the cupboard under the stairs ballooned under the weight of read newspapers, broken (but potentially fixable) gadgets and previously used Christmas wrap. The binmen must have thought our house was vacant.

Of course, as a small child, I'd largely switch off to all this. I was more interested in *Star Wars*, going out on my skateboard and then later as teen, playing in my room on a ZX81 computer. How many times do you need to hear the story about seeing a banana for the first time and having to be shown how to peel it? Every supermarket I'd ever been dragged around was drowning in them. Rightly or wrongly, I was more drawn to my two grandfathers, as both were soldiers during the First World War and like my Action Man toys, I considered them proper fighting heroes. To me, my parents, with all their tales of woe and privation, well, they were just... irritating.

As an adult, at a point when I started reflecting on my own life, I would consider my university days to be my formative years. For my parents, it was World War Two. I went drinking at the students' union bar and enjoyed lots of gigs, they crouched in garden shelters and were bombed.

Around 1990, my parents retired and moved to Ludlow in Shropshire, where they lived on fairly modest pensions and explored options to remain active whilst supplementing their incomes. This is when their war experiences came to the fore again, as they became regular after dinner speakers. During the course of a decade, they must have delivered hundreds of talks, finding a captive audience among groups such as the region's Women's Institute members. I was just pleased they were busy enjoying life. I also think that my mother's recall of such events became second nature because of all the energy she put into recounting her childhood stories. For her, they were never buried memories.

When Dad's health went downhill and he was diagnosed with Alzheimer's disease, Mum had no choice but to curtail her speaking engagements. Finding herself stranded at home and becoming a carer late in life was a difficult period for such an outgoing person. However, not one to twiddle her fingers, she turned her attention to writing and dedicated the spare room in the loft to her endeavours.

By then, I had a young family and lived a good several hours' drive away, and so my visits to Ludlow became irregular. I knew Mum was an avid writer because I picked up the task of sourcing and posting her typewriter ribbons for her old manual machine. As her fingers became less dextrous, kindly neighbours would help her change those ribbons. There came a point where she agreed to switch to an electric typewriter with larger keys, which I thought would be suitable for an older person. However, when I next paid a visit to the house, it had never made it out of the box and joined a growing pile of never used gifts, including a mobile phone. Technology was not her thing. So, I was incredibly surprised when, at the age of 80, Mum had her first book published about her experience of looking after Dad. She was absolutely thrilled to be interviewed by a national newspaper and invited to London to speak at a conference hosted by the Alzheimer's Society. She'd definitely found her old spark again.

Her publisher asked her what she was working on next. My mother didn't have the internet, and I remember showing her the images of the people she was corresponding with at the publishing house. She was shocked at how young they looked, but by then, everyone must have looked young to her.

Dad's health declined to the point where he finally went into fulltime care, and whilst that was a tragic junction to reach, it was a also release for my mother. No longer housebound, she was still fit enough to volunteer at the small local hospital, pushing a trolley around with newspapers and snacks. Really, though, what she wanted was a chance to talk to people once again, having been cocooned with Dad for the last few years. I know she enjoyed chatting to the patients, many of whom were around her age. Of course, they talked about their childhoods, and she told me what really struck her was how the folk with Shropshire childhoods had little recall of the war. Their life stories often started when they got married or commenced a career. By contrast, the few residents there who'd grown up in cities like Birmingham still talked enthusiastically about air raids and the war. I think this was a watershed moment for Mum because it drove home that her own childhood was somewhat different and not simply a shared experience that everyone in her generation had been through. She spent over five years living through the war in London and must have determined at that point that she would capture it all on paper.

More recently, when visiting Ludlow, I remember my children running around the house to let off steam after a long car drive before returning to me shrieking because the top floor writing room was full of cobwebs. Clearly, my mother could no longer manage the steep stairs. When Covid 19 struck, it was particularly unkind to older people like my mother, whose already limited social life was put on hold. I arranged cleaners and various helpers to come to the house and attend to her, but the loft room remained unused and out of bounds. During the first lockdown of the pandemic, when we spoke on the phone, the parallels with the war were obvious to her. Here was a national emergency with doom-laden nightly addresses and imposing restrictions to follow. She remained stoic about such matters. She'd had practice!

At the age of 88, when Mum needed to go into care herself, I had little choice but to take the difficult step of clearing out her house. What I found in her writing room by her now jammed-up typewriter was the manuscript for *London Can Take It*. It was all there, either typed or in handwritten notes, gathering dust. Given the state of that room, I don't think she'd written anything for several years. It was painful for me to see her final pages of handwriting, once a thing of beauty, quite scrawled and ragged. Yet, it was also an incredible gift to discover. Once I'd read her story, I rushed to see her in the care home because I was brimming with additional questions and kicked myself for not having paid more attention earlier. Sadly, her mental and physical decline had been rapid. She sat in the day room, eyes staring at the wall-mounted TV, with a vacant look on her face. I tried to prompt her with anecdotes from her own childhood, but she rather looked through me – none of it meant anything to her. Her mind had been hollowed out and those memories gone.

My mother loved a stage and an audience, and *London Can Take It* wasn't meant just for her close family. She was a witness to an important historical period and would be pleased as punch that her story can be shared with you.

Miles Bingham, 2025

Chapter 1
A Fresh Start

My earliest, rather scratchy memories are from before the war when we moved house from Edmonton to leafier Bush Hill Park in North London. Like a moving picture in my mind, I recall an uncle carrying me up a long road, pointing to a row of houses and saying, "That end one there is your new home." I was easy to carry; a small child born at just 4lbs in weight, everyone was always trying to build me up. Back in the 1930s, doctors were less keen on delivery by caesarean and so, where there were concerns over giving birth, the preferred method of the day was to starve the mother to produce a small child.

Now the film stutters and comes to a halt and silly, inconsequential things come to mind like being smacked for chipping fresh paint with a penny and travelling by train to visit Grannie on a snowy day. In my mind, I can still see our next-door neighbour hanging out their washing in the garden whilst a beautiful, multicoloured parrot perched on a stand and tilted its head, watching me.

Fast forward and I'm sitting on the kitchen table getting ready to go out. Everything smells of flour and yesterday's baking. My mother ruthlessly scrubs my knees as I wriggle in protest, and she's not listening as I try to explain how they've caught the sun before the rest of my legs. She's having none of it and finally lifts me down, bending over to give my knees one last wipe with a towel before giving me a quick kiss on the forehead.

We lived in a cul-de-sac that I can only describe as being shaped like a banjo; a perfect place for smaller children to explore safely and to play ball games. Nobody in those days worried about cars. In our house was my mother, father and big sister, Pam, who was fully eight years older than me. Years later, I heard my mother telling Aunt Pinkie that I was a mistake, until she realised that I'd overheard and repeated the same sentence, inserting the word 'surprise'.

Springtime arrived at the banjo, and I was now old enough to go out and explore. My father stood with me at the edge of our house and surveyed the area, whilst coughing up phlegm from his lungs in such a noisy manner that it drew glances from the neighbours opposite. He'd been gassed in the First World War and invalided out of the army, and more than twenty years later, he was still living with the consequences. He didn't appear to care about the racket he made – clearing your airways wasn't something that could be achieved quietly. Likewise, I didn't know any different and just accepted it as normal. Dad also had a burst eardrum in one ear and would sometimes cock his head or talk too loudly, although Mum thought he could hear perfectly well when he wanted. He also wore what was known as a toothbrush moustache – a square block across his top lip – and he had his hair slicked back and held by Brylcreem. It was a common look for men of his generation. If it wasn't for his kind blue eyes, some might say (although not to his face) the style was a little too much like that man Hitler, who was making all the headlines. Mum once told me she thought he had eyes like cornflowers. My dad wasn't one for compliments and stated in return how he thought she had eyes like two burnt holes in a blanket. His powers of description lacked a certain poetry.

Dad studied the flight of wooden steps at the back of the cul-de-sac that cut a large, manmade embankment in two, beyond which lay the Great Cambridge Road. We knew it as the Arterial Road. The railway also ran beyond the embankment. I could tell Dad was rather obsessed with the railway, as every time a steam train rumbled by on the other side there was a glint in his eye. Once, he hauled me on top of the garden shed, just so we might try and get a better look, although we could only see the billowing steam. It's funny that after only a few weeks of moving in, I got used to the rumble of the trains and hardly noticed them at all.

"Don't go up to the main road, it's dangerous," Dad instructed, assessing the scene before his voice softened, "but you can play on the embankment".

I ran off with my new sense of freedom towards the humming greenery. Edmonton remained a place of crowded, back-to-back houses and endless dirty buses, whereas this recent housing expansion in Bush Hill Park seemed more like visiting the countryside. Indeed, from the front bedroom window, we had views over the King George V playing fields. My dad was content for now and considered that he had done quite well. His own father didn't think he'd come to much when he lied about this age and joined up at the start of the First World War in 1914, in preference to working in the family rubber stamp business for a pittance. But he received a small weekly disability pension from the War Office and had built a career as an artist, regularly selling enough pictures, with a fair wind, to allow us to move to this more desirable area. He was not a fancy artist with pictures hanging in London galleries. Dad described himself as more of a 'bread and butter' artist, usually producing two or three affordable paintings a week that he could sell to shops across town. He was so skilled with his hands that he also picked up occasional commissions from his better-off customers, not just for pictures but also for graining. It was something he excelled at. I loved to hear him talk about the differences between bird's eye maple, bog oak or sycamore. He could also do gilding work, and I'd sit with him as he worked on an item. Sometimes, he would rub the brush through my hair for static before delicately transporting a small piece of gold leaf to its assigned place. And his reward was that we could now enjoy a garden large enough for flower beds and a small pond, and we had the luxury of an indoor toilet (to supplement the traditional outside one).

Whilst the railway line, the nearby connected bridge and the Arterial Road were all forbidden territory, the two sides of the embankment became my earthly paradise. Weather and parents permitting, I spent every hour I could squeeze out of the day clambering and playing there, so long as I remained in sight of the house. The larger embankment to the right was the one I liked the best because it had masses of wildflowers and crabbed old elderberry trees. The air always smelt sweet with blossom and underneath was the pungent odour of herbs, stinging nettles and wild horseradish, which Dad said we couldn't pull up because their roots went down to Australia. My regular companions were my two soft toys, Lamby Lumps and Pussy Pieces, which were made from Dad's old socks. Humble they may have been, but they shared my bed at night. The expression on the faces of other small children registered their contempt and pity, but it didn't matter to me. I never cared much for dolls, with their stiff bodies and dead, staring eyes.

The lower bough of an elderberry became a seat and the purple seeded grasses a mattress on which to lie and gaze at the sky. I learnt the names of the flowers; Ragged-robin, Queen Anne's lace, coltsfoot, and many more from illustrations in books, together with the insects they attracted, although I had not yet fully learnt to read. Mum helped me identify the various plants and advised that coltsfoot was particularly widespread because it thrived on the soot from the steam trains, which was slowly discolouring the back of our house.

I became absorbed with all the many and varied caterpillars. I loved the woolly ones with the long hair you could stroke, and I was elated when Dad made me a wooden box with airholes and a piece of sliding glass on top to keep them in. When I realised that many other children were collecting butterflies, I consciously branched out and looked for moths, feeding them their preferred leaves and watching fascinated as they went through their life cycle, breaking out into tiger moths, death's-head hawkmoths and my proudest achievement – an elephant hawk-moth. So began my lifelong interest in nature.

Dimly, I became more aware of hushed voices discussing the probability of war and whether it could ever be as bad as the last one, which was meant to have been the war to end all wars. My parents anxiously listened to the news on the radio (or wireless as we called it), shushing me when I tried to interrupt. In the background, I heard the authoritative voices but not the words of the presenters as it had nothing to do with me. War had not yet entered my vocabulary.

Becoming exasperated, I called out, "I want to listen to Children's Hour." They often had a nature study feature. Mum retired to the kitchen, and I wondered what she would make for tea.

In that late summer, a little tricycle did the rounds, coming to the banjo to sell a popular type of three-sided lolly that had me bolting for the door with my coins, although very soon that became a thing of the past and a *did that really happen?* kind of memory. Just around the corner, I would begin to understand the importance of what was to come and how it would change our lives forever.

Chapter 2
War Breaks Out, School Commences

On the morning that war was declared, the world around me went quiet as all the adults seemingly disappeared. Like everyone else, my parents' attention became fixed on their wireless set to hear what would become Neville Chamberlain's famous mournful address to the nation. Outside, the streets had emptied apart from youngsters like me, who innocently played with their scooters and skipping ropes, oblivious to events. Later, when I was called inside and told the news, it still didn't fully register. After all, nobody had died that day, no planes were flying over, and I could see no soldiers running to take cover. We'd been sliding into war over a period of some weeks, and this was just another day for me, not unlike the previous one.

That afternoon, we held a family conference in the front room. The fact we'd gathered there underlined the gravity of the situation because in those days people only used such rooms for important events. My parents discussed various 'what ifs', and I took comfort from the key reassuring messages, although they were generally directed towards my sister. I was more of a passenger, as if my opinion didn't count for much. Normally,

I could be relied on to have a view on everything and what I lacked in stature I certainly made up for in volume, although perhaps not this time. Toy soldiers and action comics weren't my cup of tea. I knew nothing of war. And so, for perhaps the first time in my short life, I just listened.

There'd been a lot of talk in the papers about how the Germans might use their large air force to bomb us, but Dad declared that we'd be safe here in the house, as it was away from the centre of London. I thought about the few occasions when I'd travelled with my parents into the heart of the city and concurred that it was a very long journey indeed. Dad seemed pleased with the fortuitous decision to have moved home when we did. "Compared to Edmonton, this is a place where we can breathe," he said.

The only positive thing about my dad having a bad chest was that he was never going to be called up to serve in the army. Usefully, he had kept his old army discharge papers in case they ever came in handy, and these showed that the medical board had categorised him as 'unfit for active duty'. In addition, Dad reminded us that Pam and I had no older brothers to worry about. He shared, by contrast, that when he and his brother had picked up rifles in the previous war, they'd given his poor mother palpitations. Our neat and tidy little family unit was surely in a better position than most and Dad reckoned we should be able to get by unscathed. I took my parents at their word, happy not to wallow in all the doom and gloom.

A little bit of everything changed each day, leaving me intrigued rather than scared. Noticeably, the arguments my parents had, usually about money, largely ceased from the day war commenced. Somehow, they parked their differences, at least for a while. My mother craved stability, and that was never going to happen with an artist for a husband. He worked away in the spare room with his oil-spattered easel and brushes, on good quality canvas if he could afford it or hardboard if money was tight. One day, when I was helping Mum in the garden with the clothesline, the weight of the washing pulled the post out of the ground to reveal a slowworm coiled around the base of the hole. Although I was keen on all creatures great and small, I drew the line at any kind of snake. My mother commented, "You don't like anything without a visible means of support," and then she added under her breath, "just like your dad".

A new government decree imposed a nightly blackout on the entire country, the idea being that not a chink of light could be seen by any aircrew from above. Feverishly observed, streetlights became redundant and not a household bulb could be switched on until every window was covered. This was achieved in my house with heavy curtains and cheap tape, all quite amateurish at the start. Things like skylights were simply daubed in black paint. Once the penny dropped and we realised this would be a permanent state of affairs, people put more effort into constructing elaborate blinds and shutters. In my view, the start of the war marked what would become a tremendous absence of colour.

More exciting for me was when our air raid siren, positioned on the Arterial Road, sounded for the first time. It sprang into life with an ear-splitting wail and everyone in our banjo of houses rushed into the street and gardens because we didn't know what else to do. In one fell swoop, the war had made us meet all our neighbours. Of course, there was nothing to see, and it was all just a test to get us acquainted to the different noises. We waited and chatted between ourselves in the late summer sunshine until the siren went off again, this time with a long, steady note. Mum studied a government leaflet that had come through the letterbox and by consensus we agreed it was the 'all clear' signal. I was singularly unimpressed. If this was war, then I couldn't see what all the fuss was about. The grown ups did their best to laugh it all off as an unnecessary exercise because surely Hitler and the Germans wouldn't be daft enough to take on Britain again. Some compromise might still be found before things really escalated. Even for my dad, with all his prior service in France and Belgium, the last war with Germany had been fought on the continent in trenches, which some people assumed would be the case again, if only the French could hold the line. Our homeland of Blighty could remain a safe place, a refuge.

The War Cabinet clearly knew better and was convinced that Germany's aircraft were the immediate menace. This led to the transformation of our high street. Public buildings became swathed in sandbags, as sweating labourers shovelled dirt into bags and stacked them several rows higher each day. I was full of endless questions. "What does this mean, Dad?" and "Why is that happening?" Stranger still was the unusual, upright, coffin-like metal boxes that sprung up on some of the main street corners. It was explained to me that if we were unfortunate enough to be bombed, these would be safe hiding places for the wardens and volunteers. These people would be expected to dart around looking for fires or people to help before returning to their protective coffins. Such things sounded absurd to me.

The other obvious change that had me arching my back were the hundreds of silver-grey barrage balloons that began decorating London's skyline. Suspended on cables as if swimming against a tide, they reminded me of my two goldfish, Bloater and Fifi. Additional air raid sirens were added on top of tall posts so that everyone could be in earshot, and we were fully prepared. Those sirens quickly became known by Londoners as 'moaning minnies'. When I asked to go and inspect the closest one to us on the Arterial Road, I rather dismissed it, thinking it looked more like a tin can turned on its side.

I was more absorbed – indeed distracted – by my new school and the opportunity to learn, explore and meet new friends of my own age. I hardly noticed the teachers and what might have been a set of government-appointed inspectors examining the roof and walls and having private conversations away from the children. As far as I was concerned, lessons and playtime continued, which all quickly felt normal to me. I loved my infant school. From the first day, I was enchanted with the sweet little orange chairs and desks and the kindly teacher in her multicoloured smock who went by the endearing name of Mrs Mundy (or Monday as I thought at the time). Some of my fellow pupils cried over being at school and away from their parents, whereas I recall throwing myself into making a plasticine model of Romulus and Remus after the teacher had told us a tale of ancient Rome. In the afternoon, I drew a picture of Moses in the bulrushes on the blue sugar paper we were given, and I was pleased when the teacher pinned it on the wall.

Quickly, we got into the morning ritual of the register. Shirley Amos, "present", Joan Bragg, "present" and then my name, Valerie Braunston. "Present" I'd yell back, and so on. In those first weeks, I'd sit upright and expectant, hoping my name might get called out a second time.

Some of us became monitors: ink monitors, milk monitors and playground monitors, although I considered I got the best job of all, which was the nature table monitor. This was right up my street. I ran a tight ship, constantly changing my displays and nagging the other children to bring in interesting specimens. My teacher drew the line when I wanted to bring in small dead mammals from the embankment.

Girls were taught basic sewing stitches on a large-holed canvas with enormous needles that had to be handed back at the end of each lesson. Likewise, the round tipped scissors that seemed by design incapable of cutting anything, let alone human flesh, were locked in a cupboard after class. Only a few children, deemed the most sensible, were allowed to collect up such items for the teacher. The rest of us must have been identified as having a high probability of tripping up. Having said that, I did have an unfortunate mishap drinking from the water fountain for the first time, which led me to running to the teacher with a sopping wet uniform. So maybe I wasn't to be trusted with a pair of scissors after all.

"Who'd like to come to the front and perform a dance or sing a song?" asked Mrs Mundy, wanting someone to fill in for a few minutes.

My hand shot up first. The fact I didn't possess a melodic voice and hadn't yet started any dance classes didn't deter me one iota. I had yet to discover the fine line between being keen and simply showing off, and I don't think I fully have since.

I recall being quite upset at the end of each day when we were told to go home, and I trudged towards my mother waiting to collect me at the gate. I'd have happily stayed for hours longer.

My mother was a thin-faced lady with naturally curly hair. She was nine years younger than my dad, although you wouldn't have guessed that. She blamed it on the lack of help she got from my father when both Pam and I had been born. He adored Pam, but like most men of his age, Dad wasn't at all hands-on in the early stages of childcare. When Pam had suffered from colic and cried through the night, he would say, "I've got a living to get" and turn over in bed and put the pillow over his ears. My mother told me that story on multiple occasions as a lesson, or possibly as a warning.

I think most women of that period were older than their actual years, as keeping a household running was a hard life. On washing days, the copper was forever on the boil, so the windows ran with condensation and my mother's hands would be red and swollen from handwashing and mangling. Wash day was then followed by a further day dedicated to ironing.

There was a time, early in my school life, when Mum collected me, and I could immediately tell from her alabaster white face that something was wrong. As we walked the short distance home, she broke the news to me. "Your Dad and I have decided that Pam should be evacuated," she said. I looked at my mother with sheer bewilderment. Her voice quivered. "It won't be for too long, but I think you're too young to go, so you'll stay back with us."

In that moment, I was both relieved and happy that my life wasn't about to be turned upside down. On reflection, I may have even been a little pleased that my sister was being sent away. It wasn't that I didn't love Pam, but we were like chalk and cheese, and the age difference between us was obvious. Sometimes, it felt like I was an only child because she rarely wanted to play with me. I often spent hours alone throwing a tennis ball against the side of the house to entertain myself, forwards and downwards and then under my legs. This routine usually came to grief when I tried a full turn before catching it. Pam was allowed to do things forbidden to me such as cross the main road or stay up late. On the other hand, she thought our parents were soft with me because I was small and the youngest. The rivalry must have been tiresome for my parents who had enough on their plates. When Mum was busy, she would ask my sister to keep an eye on me, which meant Pam lugging me about when she went to hang around with her friends at the top of the road. I didn't care much for them, as they mostly ignored me. They would talk about boys and who looked good in uniform and other things I wasn't particularly interested in. I'd sometimes hear people refer to Pam as lovely or even beautiful, whereas I might be described as quaint. I didn't really know what quaint meant, although I sensed it wasn't as good as beautiful. Without meaning to, I always got in Pam's way with her friends. If she caught me listening to something I shouldn't have heard, she would tug me by my pigtails, warning me on the way home to "keep my mouth shut".

I'd been so caught up in my own school life that I'd failed to realise that half of the schools in the area plus their teachers had already left for places like Norfolk, and it had been touch and go as to whether Pam would go with the first wave. My parents had probably been discussing it for a long time and had held on, wanting to keep the family together, but there was a lot of pressure on all the parents to get the children away from danger. Posters had gone up screaming out the instruction, *Mothers, let them go.*

Anyway, when it was Pam's scheduled time to leave, we all kissed her goodbye as she boarded one of a fleet of red double decker buses laid on specially for the trip. They quickly filled with children, each one with a brown tag tied to them so they all looked like parcels awaiting delivery. As the vehicles pulled away, their faces pressed against the glass windows full of wonder at the adventures ahead of them. Everyone waved enthusiastically.

As soon as we got back home, like any other annoying little sister, I raided Pam's bedroom to see what toys and books she'd left behind. I had to make the most of the opportunity, given I'd been told she'd be back before I knew it. Yet, every night for a week after Pam left, I was disturbed hearing my mother crying in her bedroom, and always there was my father with his stumbling attempts to comfort her.

Once Pam and the others left for Norfolk in that second wave of evacuations, the banjo became as quiet as a chapel. With a lack of playmates, the biggest immediate change for me was that I had to develop the skill of spending long stints of time on my own, amusing myself. It also meant I ended up listening in more to grown up conversations and picking up their expressions, even if I didn't always follow the meaning.

Pam soon became a regular writer, and it was always an upbeat day when a letter from her arrived. It all sounded like one great adventure. She was quick to let us know how happy she was and how she had a playmate of around her age named

Poppy. I thought Poppy was the prettiest name I'd ever heard and vowed that if I had a little girl one day she'd be called Poppy Rose. I know Pam really enjoyed her time away and she kept in touch with her 'foster' family for many years after the war. One story she did tell me later was that whilst she was in Norfolk, she started her menstrual period, which nobody had prepared her for. With no prior warning or knowledge, she thought she'd injured herself climbing a tree and went to ask her foster parents for advice on what to do. If ever a girl needed her mother, it was then. Such was the life of an evacuee.

Back in Bush Hill Park, I couldn't see why everyone was either leaving London or talking about evacuation, as absolutely nothing had happened to endanger us. "It's just precautionary," everyone would say. Tripping over a sandbag and cracking open my skull seemed the most imminent threat. Anyway, I had other things on my mind. I'd persuaded some of the last remaining children living nearby to accompany me one Saturday morning under the railway bridge, so we could explore further. I knew I wasn't supposed to wander, but my conscience was clear because we wouldn't go on the actual railway line or to the main road, which were the areas Dad had been specific about. Also, now that hostilities had commenced, the grown ups appeared preoccupied, meaning I was less likely to be observed.

I remember it was dark under the bridge itself, and we were smitten by the little pools of water congregated there that had seemingly never seen daylight. The most exciting thing was rushing back under the bridge to huddle as a fire-spitting dragon of a train thundered over our heads. Collecting ourselves, we emerged into the light on the other side and quickly discovered a vast grassy area that we later learnt were the County School playing fields. On the edge of a nearby pitch by a school building, we spotted a delightful, fully grown weeping willow tree. Once inside its long, drooping branches, we found ourselves in a heavenly circular room where shards of sunlight pierced the canopy and patterned the earth at our feet. In such moments, life couldn't have been much better.

We returned the next day with our arms full of old cushions. Someone had brought a blanket, from which we made a little den. We christened our new home Willow Cottage and visited several times when the weather was on our side to laze away our free time, eat dripping sandwiches and tell each other stories. There were still no bombers overhead or search lights raking the sky, or any other such things that were soon to become part of our daily existence.

Chapter 3

Gas Masks at the Ready

The issuing of gas masks to every person in the country was like a terrible hangover from the First World War. With Hitler such an unknown quantity, people feared the horror of a gas attack upon the civilian population above anything else. Dad was under no illusion, and I sensed a resigned sadness in him as he hung my own gas mask over my shoulder.

"Forget all your toys," he said. "From now on, *this* is your single most important possession, and it is to be kept with you at *all* times."

They also took it very seriously at school and regularly drove home the exact same message. Unfortunately, not long before I received my own mask and box case, I'd had four baby teeth extracted by the dentist. Being such a chatterbox from a young age, I think my parents used to keep me quiet as a toddler with handfuls of penny sweets, and I was now paying the price. Not that anyone had warned me what was about to happen. To take with us to the dentist appointment, Mum had dug out my old pushchair from the cupboard under the stairs. I was so naïve that I didn't think to ask why. At the surgery, I sat with eight equally nervous children. One by one they trooped through the door to where the dentist was operating, and I heard all their cries and screams as they underwent treatment. Being the very last patient to go in, I'd seen all their pasty faces emerge, spitting blood and crying for their mothers. When it was my time, I was led in by a nurse who announced in an overly bright voice, "The last one is always the bravest," which really put me on my guard.

The room had an unpleasant, medical-like aroma and was attended by two middle-aged men, who were masked and in white coats. They started off trying to be jolly and saying things like, "Let's have a little look inside," before they attempted to put a giant rubber mask on my face. It smelt like the inside of a hot water bottle, and I immediately started to panic, at which point they became quite forceful. I must have succumbed to the ether as I don't remember any more of the procedure. And when I awoke, I was ensconced in my old pushchair and rather grateful for it, feeling no shame at being wheeled down the street in my woozy state. In my hand I had one of my dad's hankies, which I clutched tightly against my numb mouth as it slowly turned from white to red.

On the way home, my mum confessed that she'd had most of her teeth extracted at the age of twenty when she was expecting Pam. That didn't exactly sell the idea of motherhood to me.

So, when it came to my first gas mask practice at school, the first sniff of that sweet, rubbery odour transported me straight back to the dentist's chair, though my teachers had no intention of indulging my whims that morning.

"Stop throwing your head around like a funeral horse," instructed the teacher, as she tried to hold my head still and yank the straps tight on this one-size-fits-all item.

After we were all present and correct, another teacher marched up and down our line holding a piece of paper against the filter nozzle on each mask to ensure that air was being drawn in and out correctly. The masks were notoriously tricky to breathe through, at least until you got used to them. As my eye holes misted up, I waited for a child to collapse from asphyxiation. It was a blessed relief to finally be told we could take off our masks, although I attempted this too hastily and the device took some of my flesh away with it. Like most of my classmates, I spent the rest of the day with big red strap marks around my face.

It got marginally better with each successive practice, as we got used to breathing in them correctly. I remember we were taught a long rhyming ditty called 'Beware Gas' that was meant to help us to identify different types of gas, and it was regularly sung once our masks had been packed back in their boxes. The first verse went:

"If you get a choking feeling

And a smell of musty hay,

You can bet your bottom dollar

That there's phosgene on the way."

And so on. What a jolly song for small children! There must have been lots of poisonous gases out there as the rhyme went on forever.

When a classmate discovered that you could make a particularly rude noise by blowing hard and forcing air out of the rubber sides, we practically trampled over our teachers to form a queue the next time we were instructed to get ready for practice. They quickly became frustrated at our antics. Never being able to pinpoint the culprit, they shouted at us all in increasingly shrill voices about all the grizzly ways we might die from gas poisoning if we didn't take things seriously.

After that, the number of drills reduced, and it became more a matter of ensuring every pupil had their mask to hand. All this took place alongside our normal lessons, and it quickly became a regular part of school life, and for me, nothing particularly out of the ordinary. In the same vein, I had little awareness of the teaching staff changing around me. Men continued to join up in their droves and many greying teachers were forced to delay or to even begrudgingly come out of retirement to form a scratch staff. The whole country was shifting on the tectonic plates of war, but I was still too young to fully absorb what was happening.

In this period of drills and practice, before any of the actual bombing started, it was still acceptable to travel, and so we continued to visit our relatives (everyone back then had big extended families). Most travel was by train and then bus or foot. We didn't own a car, and at that point in my life, I still hadn't been in one. Even for those people fortunate enough to possess a vehicle, there was practically no petrol to buy as it had been one of the first things to be rationed.

On this occasion, my parents took me to the house of the wonderfully named Aunt Pinkie. I had many aunties in my life, but it was all somewhat confusing, as I gradually discovered that many of them weren't the genuine article, but instead were only my mother's friends. Aunt Pinkie was a plump, jolly lady with tiny feet and large breasts. Mum believed she had the knack of being able to stop any baby crying because they could snuggle into her bosom and feel secure. As a small child, I was always allowed to explore the house, and I remember being mesmerised by her bedroom because it was all green. There was a green carpet and a green silk bedspread as well as a collection of emerald trinkets on her dressing table that caught the sunlight and threw the most interesting patterns across her walls. Mum suspected that it must be like living underwater, but I loved it.

At these gatherings, I would sometimes get frustrated at being dragged around to be introduced to this or that family member. In my simple world, I decided a real aunt was someone who bought you birthday or Christmas presents and those who didn't weren't blood relations. It was a bit arbitrary, yet the reasoning worked for me.

Whilst my aunts were all kind to me, my uncles were more of a mixed bag. I considered them slightly shadowy figures, who smelled of beer and tobacco but were good for the odd sixpence if you caught them at the right moment. The one that particularly interested me, because we'd never met, was my dad's brother, Uncle Phil. I'd heard enough from the adults to know that he'd been involved in some sort of scandal and my ears always pricked up when his name was mentioned (Mum sometimes called me a nosy parker). I'd pieced together that when he'd joined up in the First World War alongside my father, some sort of serious wrongdoing had led Uncle Phil to abscond from the British Army and run away to Canada. After the war, Phil had remained abroad, and he could never return to Britain for fear of arrest. Even at a young age, I enjoyed such a delicious intrigue.

Alcohol was usually central to these family parties. There'd be bottles of brown ale for the men and maybe a sherry for the ladies. The older ones often drank quite a lot. Even for those out of a job or supposedly hard up, there'd always be money for more drink. I'd hang around my mother, holding on to her dress and generally getting in the way of people. I recall there were few other children to play with due to the evacuations.

Lots of homes had a piano and such events would often descend into a regular sing-along. I'd hear someone clank two glasses together and appeal for everyone to gather around. This time, Uncle Fred took up his usual position by the piano and gave us his rendition of 'Come into the Garden, Maud'. His voice rose towards the final line in a strangulated tenor – "I am here at the gate aaa-lone" – and when I caught Mum's eye, we both had to look away to control our fits of giggling.

I knew my dad wasn't so keen on the singing and I went looking for him in the next room. He wasn't hard to spot. His rattling cough gave him away before I saw him silhouetted behind a fog of pipe and cigarette smoke in the middle of a huddle of men. Dad smoked twenty Senior Service a day (or Senior Citizens as I mistakably called them) and blamed it all on his time in the trenches and the free cigarettes given out by the army. He revealed just about everyone in uniform had smoked. Surrounded by family and friends, everyone knew my dad and made allowances as he hacked up his lungs in public, although woe betide anyone foolish enough to suggest he should give up his smokes.

Not to be left out, my mother was also a heavy smoker, and once, when she'd lit up in front of me, I'd asked her, "Were you in the trenches as well?" This brought on one of my dad's more laboured coughing fits. He waved me away, as he tried to stop laughing, padding his breast pocket for his lighter.

Of course, the conversation at the party centred around the war – what was happening, who had joined up and who was doing essential war work that meant they wouldn't be called up. Dad was in the centre of things being quizzed about the last war, as at the time, it was the only point of reference people had. You could divide the men roughly into those under forty, with their puppy-dog enthusiasm for taking on Hitler, versus the old salts who'd been in uniform during the previous war. My dad had little time for these young men with their bum fluff moustaches, as he described them. Like most men who had already served, he remained fairly impenetrable on the subject, although that didn't stop him from tossing into the debate the odd hand grenade.

"Any silly beggar with a dose of patriotic fervour should try spending a week under fire," he'd say. "That'll soon cure them."

My dad was never concerned about ruffling a few feathers, although there was a hum of agreement from the middle-aged men. It would've been hard to find a male in their forties who wasn't shaped, physically or mentally, by their service in the prior war.

"Still, every day is jam," he'd add with a shrug and a smile, recognising that he'd dampened the mood. This was one of my father's favourite expressions and it reflected his joy at being alive after surviving the trenches. Possibly, it was one of the few of his phrases that didn't involve swearing.

Despite his injuries, he considered that he was one of the lucky ones. He impressed on me that he couldn't believe people wanted to repeat those terrible events all over again in some form of collective amnesia.

Then at Aunt Pinkie's house, when the war talk was over and the drinks had been flowing, I found myself isolated with someone called Uncle Harry that I hardly knew – no presents, so not a real uncle. He amused himself by supplying me with boiled sweets while teasing me at the same time, and I was happy to put up with his nonsense for anything sugary. When I seemed to irritate him by asking a question about Phil and Canada, I distinctly heard him say something about "you lot", and then he announced clearly, "You're not even a Braunston."

"What do you mean, Uncle Harry?" I asked in response to such as strange sentence, holding his gaze whilst looking for an explanation.

"You're a Braun*stein*," he replied, crudely emphasising the ending. He then dismissed me with a wave of his hand, his eyes searching for another bottle of ale. "Don't ask me, go and ask your parents."

*

It was early evening by the time we left for home, and due to the pervasive blackout, we walked with caution until needing to cross the road, a task that demanded our full attention. Nobody but a bat would venture out after dark without a torch. And so, I held on to the questions gathered in my head. As our bus approached, I could hear it well before it came into view. Casting an eerie beam due to its front lights taped and dampened, the bus arrived out of the gloom with the slits of cats' eyes. As it pulled away, moving stealthily between each stop, the only internal lighting came from some dim blue bulbs, and there was barely enough to see the nearest face with any clarity. The traffic on the roads appeared to be mostly army transports. I parked myself next to Mum whilst Dad sat on the seat in front, and once the bus conductor had moved on, those questions spilled out of me.

"Am I adopted, or something worse?"

My parents exchanged glances and when they spoke, Uncle Harry quickly transformed into "that bloody man". In a noticeably hushed voice, Dad turned and leaned over from his seat to explain that his surname used to be Braunstein but he changed it when he joined the army in 1914, years before he'd met my mother. "It was too Jewish sounding," he disclosed as if I would fully understand.

My voice tightened as I swivelled towards Mum. "So, are we Jewish, then?" I didn't want to raise my voice in any way, as from their reaction, it felt as though I'd revealed an awkward secret.

"No, dear," Mum replied firmly, adding, "and another reason he changed his name was because it sounded too German."

"Please don't tell me we are German?" I hissed under my breath.

"No, don't be silly, we're definitely not German. We're not really... anything," she replied with a deadpan face.

The conversation was clearly over as both of my parents turned away to stare out of their respective windows, even though it was total darkness outside. I remained confused by all the half-explanations. If I wasn't 'anything' then I was a nothing. I didn't understand how you could just alter your name and whether that was allowed, or if I liked being a nothing.

When I got home, I gazed into the mirror at my deep brown eyes, traced my jet-black, bushy eyebrows with a finger and rearranged my unruly dark plaits. For the first time, I missed my sister, as I'm sure she'd have been able to explain things to me. Pam also had dark, straight hair and sweeping black eyelashes that framed her large, grey-blue eyes. My dad had remarked that we were "well marked kittens". At that point, I started questioning whether I was like those children that Pam had told me about who were allowed to stand to the side at her school assembly each day before the Christian hymns were sung. For the first time, whilst I wanted to be like everyone else, I started to feel a little bit... separated. It was like I was a jigsaw piece that wouldn't quite fit into the intended gap.

Chapter 4
The Ugly Intruder

It was a significant event when Anderson shelters were delivered to each house on the banjo one grey morning. The war had arrived on my front step. The few remaining children on the estate, mostly young ones like me, excitedly ran about whilst my parents and neighbours came onto the street to observe proceedings. Labourers jumped off the back of the large truck, pulled up their shirt sleeves and then heaved equipment into individual piles outside each house. Similar shelters had already gone up closer to Central London, in what were considered high risk areas. We'd seen it in the newspapers. The fact that this was deemed necessary for our leafy suburb was a little more disturbing.

The shelters didn't arrive complete but were rather a kit that made the basis for a homemade shelter. My mother was aghast at the thought that part of her newly established garden was about to be ruined.

The remaining men in our street were expected to help out, particularly with the elderly who wouldn't be able to manage the task of construction. Back then, most men were good with their hands and owned tools, and so for several days you could hear much digging, sawing and hammering, plus some occasional bad language. A healthy competition developed between neighbours as to the best shelter, with a few aching backs to follow. On the banjo, we all had reasonably sized gardens and could manage the construction. Those people without outside space had to wait for Morrison shelters, which were essentially a steel, table-shaped cage for indoor use that you could hide inside.

Our Anderson shelter was made of corrugated, galvanized steel panels bolted to an angled iron frame. It was necessary to install it over the top of a hole, to be dug several feet deep. Dad resolutely got on with the task of digging a pit in the garden as a start point. I decided to sit on a chair in the garden and keep him company. He stuck his finger into the soil in several places and muttered things to no one in particular about the water table and the London clay, before making some necessary adjustments. It must have been a long time since he'd helped dig trenches or made dugouts, although he certainly gave the impression that he had some expertise when it came to holes in the ground.

"The shovel has always been a soldier's best friend," he mused, taking a breather and using his boot to clean off some mud clinging to the base of his spade. "It will keep you out of trouble. But the real secret to a good dugout is the finishing touches like boarding the floor so we can avoid wet feet."

I nodded in agreement at his sage words until it felt as if my head might fall off. I definitely didn't want soggy feet.

Dad returned to his task, and slowly but surely, the hole in our garden spread. I hadn't really seen my dad labouring like that before. Other people's fathers did manual work or went to factories every day, whilst I grew up knowing that mine was different. The other fathers got up and left their homes at the same time each morning, shuffling off to the trains and buses and increasingly heading for coach stops laid on to take workers to factories doing war work. I could hear the characteristic clip clop sound they all made leaving the banjo, because as new shoes became harder to source, people had taken to fitting steel Blakey's onto their soles to stop them wearing out.

My father was a man who didn't want to toe the line. He did things his own way. Sometimes, as I got ready for school downstairs, my first view of Dad was of him wandering around the house in a dressing gown keeping 'artists' hours', as he called them. Over time, I realised that I was lucky to have him around. Some of my friends had strained relationships with their fathers, something made even worse once they were called away to the war.

Dad had been a self-employed artist since convalescing in Essex after the First World War, where he discovered the Southend School of Art. And so, a hobby became a trade. He painted large landscapes and seascapes in oils of places he'd rarely been and ships he'd never sailed on. I considered that he must have had a remarkable imagination.

Other friends in the art community visited on occasion and they stood out with their slightly non-regulation dress sense or longer cut of hair, the sort that might attract raised eyebrows from onlookers. I also noticed that they called my dad 'Len'. In fact, my father's full name was Horace Leonard Braunston, which is how he signed each of his paintings. He'd been given the name Horace after Horatio Nelson on account of being born on Trafalgar Day, which was a significant historical date at the time. Understandably, he'd never liked the name Horace, and who can blame him? Even in the 1940s, it was considered a bit fusty, and so he often went by Len to friends whilst he was Horace to his family. It was another name muddle with my dad.

Our house was full of vibrant clipper ships cutting through the waves and snow-covered alpine vistas, and our new house gave Dad a whole room he could use as a studio thanks to its large windows and good daylight. My mother loved his pictures and enjoyed hanging them in the house when they were finished, although to my father it was work and they were items to sell. Whenever people asked him how he could part with his art, he'd chastise them, pointing out that an artist with a house full of his own pictures wasn't selling very well.

*

It took two days to complete the external structure of our Anderson shelter, and throughout that period, Mum kept supplying Dad with endless cups of tea, something still plentiful and not yet rationed. Clearly, she was less interested in Dad's parched throat and her real intention was to inspect the work.

"Please don't trample on the surrounding flower beds," she implored, almost dancing on the spot.

Dad scratched his head and replied unconvincingly, "I'll do what I can."

Despite his best intentions, Dad couldn't always help where he stepped, and by the time he'd shovelled all the excavated soil in a bank around the sides of the structure, Mum's flower beds were largely flattened. On top, our shelter was then covered with the final left-over earth in a mound, not to disguise it, but to give it extra protection. The entrance was a square, cut-out hole in the centre at ground level, with a hinged door facing the house. It had to be crawled through, which made it great fun to a small child because it was so easy for me. On the inside was a piece of thick sacking to pull back across the entrance to prevent any light from escaping. This also provided an added barrier against any gas.

My mum took great pride in the garden and resented the ugly intruder as another imposition brought on by the war. She endeavoured to disguise it by piling up additional soil, stones and rock plants until Dad begged her to stop, saying that we were more in danger from a landslide of aubretia than from a stray bomb. Mum had the last laugh, however, because the next day we heard a mechanical digger in the field opposite and Dad rushed upstairs to see what was happening from the top floor window. The finely cut grass of the King George V playing field, my dad's idea of countryside after a life in Edmonton, was being dug up and converted into emergency allotments.

"I didn't pay £100 extra for this house just so I could look at beans and cabbages," my dad spat out in exasperation. He refused to put his name down for an allotment out of principal, although he later tried to claim that being outside in all weathers wouldn't have been good for his chest. I found this all quite amusing and didn't twig why it might be important to grow our own food. Soon, 'Dig for Victory' would become a well-known call to action. Even the lawns outside the Tower of London would become vegetable patches to show that we were all in it together.

Inside our shelter, Dad had knocked together four basic bunk beds, just a shoulder's width between the rows, with steel spring mesh tops on which bedding, or a single mattress, could be laid. I was happy to see the shelter as an additional playhouse, although I disliked the idea that we might eventually have to sleep in such a construction. Once inside, I had a sensation of being partially buried underground. Fortunately, not a single bomb had yet targeted British civilians and I was able to push any concerns to the back of my mind.

The good news was that our Anderson shelter attracted a stray cat that turned up on a winter's day, begging for a home. To my delight, probably because my parents were seeking anything to lighten the mood, they agreed to let me keep her, and so the cat joined our household, and we called her Sandy. This was a jolly lucky cat as many people had made the hard decision in recent weeks to have their own pets euthanised.

"Someone didn't have the heart to put her down," speculated Dad. "That's one of her nine lives used up."

I couldn't see how keeping cats and dogs would undermine the country's fight against the Germans. Sandy looked a complete mess from sleeping rough and, as Mum said, it was hardly love at first sight, but we gave her some scraps and she quickly became part of our family. Even after food and a good brush, she still looked like a bit of a bruiser with a split left ear, one eye partially closed and a meow like a rusty gate.

Sandy quickly established herself as the terror of the neighbourhood and refused to countenance any other cats in our garden. In the evenings, under the blackout, we would hear her blood curdling cries and yowls, and sure enough, the next day, she would reappear with another scratch or a tuft of fur missing.

However much our family wanted to avoid the war, certain situations were out of our control. My father kept plugging away with his art, although the war had put a slow stranglehold on his earnings. He was never precious about his talent and would walk around London with several pictures under his arm, taking them to shops and galleries to sell. That was where the hard graft came in. He would never part with his work on a 'sale or return' basis. He demanded cash on the nail, saying that shops couldn't source a table, or a bone china tea set without paying for them upfront. However, it wasn't an easy living. One of the worst effects of the blackouts, particularly now winter was upon us, were that many of his shop customers commenced shutting early. It was surprising how darkness could fall on such a big city like London. This, combined with the shortages of goods and foodstuffs, meant some retailers stopped opening altogether.

Dad was having a thin time of it and increasingly, he returned home still laden with the same number of canvases that he'd left with in the morning. He sometimes wore a grim expression that we called his 'bug mouth', and we knew to tread carefully around him those evenings. My parents, once again, started arguing about money issues. You couldn't blame the public for pulling their horns in. Who'd want to buy a luxury item like a picture when your house faced being wrecked by German bombs?

One day, I found my dad slumped in his chair, an unfinished picture on the easel. He seemed to be staring at his work, or was it the wall? He looked browbeaten, even a little crushed. In those difficult times, he was forced to find the only work available to a man with a paintbrush and started assisting shopkeepers to paint their spare windows black. His life swiftly went from colour and imagination to turning the world dark.

Chapter 5
Losing Your Marbles

Whilst the war's broader effect started to impinge on our family, the fighting remained very much at arm's length, as we had the RAF defending our skies. Our main connection was through the wireless broadcasts that my parents religiously listened to in the evenings to keep up to date. I was aware that battles were taking place and lives were being lost, yet it was all happening somewhere else. During those early days of what was soon to become known as the 'Battle of Britain', when a single life still mattered, I heard in a broadcast for the first time the words, "One of our planes is missing." I wish I could say that I understood or appreciated the Herculean efforts made by our pilots at the time or how pivotal they were in staving off invasion. My parents continued to shelter me from the worst of the war, and with the self-centredness of the young, I still thought the world revolved around me and my day-to-day needs.

The first war-related death I was aware of and that upset me was of the parrot next door. The poor thing had apparently died because its owners couldn't source the right type of bird food any longer. We would never hear it say, "Baldie, light the fire" to its owner ever again. On the wireless, we often listened to a much-requested talking budgerigar that had the name Beauty Metcalfe and who used to say, "Good God, look at the time" as clear as anything. Given keeping the masses happy had become of prime importance, I expect she enjoyed endless amounts of the right food!

My parents keenly wanted my life to remain as normal as possible, which meant attending school every day, and I was quite content with that. I was always happier in company. It had been a touch-and-go situation for a while as to whether all the city's schools should close for the war's duration, but common sense prevailed and most around my way remained open in some shape or form. However, the rhythm of school life became increasingly interrupted by events. We regularly had air raid practice, which meant filing out to the corridor in an orderly fashion whilst our teachers would command, "No running, please." Presumably, we were being led away from the windows. It was never explained as we were deemed too young. We then had to sit in the corridor positioned with our backs to the wall. Often, we were in the semi-darkness as there was a lack of natural light, so it was all quite tedious. I remember the teacher would read us stories or play her recorder to entertain us until we were dismissed.

Air raid practice was not to be confused with the fire drills, which entailed going into the playground without a coat whatever the weather and waiting in the open to be counted. It was hammered into me that bombs meant being inside and fires meant we should go outside. In the scenario where bombs were dropping and fires were starting, it wasn't evident what we were meant to do.

Air raid sirens went off on occasion, even though we hadn't seen or heard many planes, and we considered most to be false alarms. All the fighting in the sky was taking place over the ports or around the RAF airfields. If the 'all clear' signal didn't follow, our parents were allowed to come and collect us, or indeed a whole string of children if they lived in the same street. Mercifully, we hadn't the experience or imagination to envisage what might happen in a real raid, and most of us were just happy to skip a lesson or two.

On another day early in the war, when I arrived at school, all the windows had been crisscrossed with strips of a sticky, gauze anti-blast tape. The task must have been completed overnight. Until I got used to it, it felt like I was sitting inside a prison. There were also workmen at the far end of the playground that day, hastily slapping up a thick, squat brick shelter. Such shelters were meant to be impervious to everything bar a direct hit, although we didn't always use ours and there was a debate about the safest place for us to go in the event of a real bombing.

If the Germans or a fire weren't going to kill us, then the school milk surely would. The milk bottles each held a third of a pint, and come rain or shine were delivered in crates and unceremoniously dumped at the gravelled area by the side of the main school building. In winter, the bottles might be full of crystals, although the warm days were worse because refrigeration was not yet common. I hated it. The teachers got us to form lines to receive our milk, even when the sun was beating down, and we were regularly forced to drink it when it was 'on the turn'. The teacher would get really cross if I displayed any reluctance. She would extol the cure-all virtues of milk, tell me not to be so fussy and to get it down. To this day, since the war, I've never been able to stomach drinking a glass of milk.

Our health remained a major concern to the grown-ups. On an annual basis, we were seen by a school doctor and a parent had to be present in case the conversation needed to be more serious. When it came to my turn, the doctor tried to put a spatula down my throat, which made me gag. As I did so, my arm went up in a spontaneous movement and I almost took his eye out with my fingernails. It caused quite a commotion, and the doctor was none too pleased. "This child has tonsils like half a pound of raw beef!" he said.

I think he would have had my tonsils out on the spot if there'd been a scalpel in his medical bag. Fortunately, my mother didn't want bits of me chopped off unless absolutely necessary, and so I avoided that imposition.

Every so often, we were also inspected by the school nurse, who would weigh us and take notes, although I got the sense she was particularly interested in the state of our hair and what we might be harbouring there. The nurse had a field day with my long black locks and looked particularly disappointed when she failed to discover any little visitors. Everyone in the class fell about laughing when one girl returned to class and triumphantly announced, "I passed my inspection. She only found a few nits in my fringe."

Apart from those minor irritations, I was wholly in favour of school and wondered why Pam had always made such a fuss about hers in the past. We were counting beads as we learnt rudimentary maths, which progressed to simple adding and subtracting. Sometimes, I would come unstuck, as I was loath to disturb a pretty pattern I'd created with my coloured beads. Later, we moved on to learning tables by rote. I also remember the class reading a simplified version of *Toad of Toad Hall* by A. A. Milne. I'm not sure how it happened, but reading came to me as naturally as breathing.

It wasn't long before I reinforced my reputation as a show off. A daily poetry recital gave me another opportunity to step to the front of class and please my teacher, although I was really only pleasing myself. I didn't understand why so many of the others held back or were afraid of going to the front of the class. I'd found an audience and revelled in it.

At some point in those early school days, we were divided into groups, and the more able pupils were instructed to help the others in class. That led to me being awarded my own small group to look after, which proved to be quite a mistake because I had no patience with them when they read aloud, and I could barely contain myself if they stumbled or emphasised the wrong word. Looking back, I must have been insufferable. When my mother came into the school, my form teacher told her that I was precocious for my age, kept everyone on their toes and would benefit from a volume dial. I had little idea that I was perceived as such a menace. Twisting in her seat, Mum tried to explain that our whole family tended to talk rather loudly in order to make themselves heard.

When it came to an enforced daily rest period, given my obvious weakness for talking in class, I found the whole exercise a great trial. We were meant to fold our arms on the tables and place our heads down until Miss Mundy shouted, "Wake up, everyone." I couldn't just switch on and off to order, and so I was always being ticked off. This once led to me being sent to the headmistress, and I recall entering her study with a thumping heart. Fortunately, she seemed quite amused by me, and after a pleasant getting-to-know-you conversation, she pointed out that if the whole class behaved like me then we would never get any work done.

Everyone loved break time, and one of our favourite pastimes was playing with our skipping ropes. This soon developed into a communal playground game whereby a long rope was stretched the width of the playground with two strong girls wildly turning it at each end. You would queue up to leap in the middle and stay for as long as possible before relinquishing your place to the next girl. Of course, the oldest girls were much better than the little ones, and after a while we'd gather and watch them compete. The rhyme I remember them chanting as they skipped went, "Play up Millwall, can't play football." They executed bumps on the final syllables, which meant letting the rope pass under them twice whilst they remained in the air. We could only watch and admire their athleticism.

In our playground, by some osmosis known only to schoolchildren, games changed overnight. Skipping ropes gave way to another game called 'Whip and Top'. We all had one and the idea was to keep the top spinning for as long as possible with the aid of the whip. It was customary to make our tops as decorative as possible, because of the mesmerising visual effect of them when they were spun at speed. I forget who came up with the idea of fixing a milk bottle top with a drawing pin to their top, but we all followed the fashion, and very pretty they looked too.

It wasn't all play, and with so many parents away in uniform or waiting to sign up, there was always plenty of hearsay on the war, particularly as we circulated around the bigger children in the playground. With the war progressing, the children quickly picked up on whose dad was serving, and where. There was even bleak gossip about who was surely going to get killed. On more than one occasion, a girl would be in tears because her father had just been called up that morning or because some mean child predicted that they'd soon be a 'goner'. The snarliest of comments were reserved for those children whose fathers had found a cushy job that meant they would remain tucked away at home. In the courtroom of the playground, there was no greater sin.

"My dad has still got shrapnel in his back from Vimy Ridge in the first war," reported a girl in our class called Joan Bragg, wanting to put the record straight.

"Well, my dad was shot on the Somme and has a metal plate in his head," declared someone else in a slightly grotesque form of one-upmanship.

"Liar," chorused several girls who obviously knew different and declared he was perfectly healthy and worked as a bank manager.

I pushed forward, not wanting people to think my dad was a shirker. "He can't join up because he was hospitalised by mustard gas at... Pash-en-dale." Although a mouthful to pronounce, such placenames like the Somme and Passchendaele already had a mythical status and were as familiar to many schoolchildren as any nearby town.

"Bet he wasn't, and you can't even spell the place," shouted one of the meaner girls.

"He was too," I shot back, jabbing a finger her way. "When they shipped him home, he was forced to eat *raw* liver sandwiches for *six* months."

This shut them up, as I'd be too young to make up something like that. I was glad there were no other questions though, as I'd nearly exhausted my scant knowledge of Dad's wartime tribulations and hadn't a clue what raw liver had to do with mustard gas. To me, it sounded like a roast dinner gone badly wrong. The more belligerent girls headed off, and I calmed myself fiddling with the marbles in my blazer pocket, enjoying their tactile nature.

Marbles were another universal pastime, and everyone had pockets full of them. We swapped and traded them each day like a currency. I was completely obsessed with their beauty: velvet brown ones, milky blue ones, clear ones with a spiral in the middle and multicoloured ones like smaller versions of the paperweights I'd seen at my relatives' houses. I loved them all and hated losing any in the games we played. Turns were taken to flick a marble into a small hole, such as a drain cover, and the person who nudged their marble closest to the centre spot won the lot.

If I lost a prized jewel from my collection, Mum would sing to me an old folk song called 'Johnny's Lost His Marbles', to try and placate me. That was all very well, but as the war progressed, any lost marbles became harder to replace. Sometimes, I'd cry myself to sleep over them.

Our school break times were staggered, yet there was a period of cross over when the older pupils loitered nearby. Like a pack of wolves, they descended on our game of marbles, knowing that with their superior reflexes and coordination, there were easy pickings to be had.

Having learnt my lesson, I could see what was coming and so pocketed my favourite marbles, only willing to risk the more common ones. In my class circle, my friend Janet Woodgate was slower than most and foolishly agreed to play with her best ones, only to swiftly lose the lot.

From her kneeled position, she scrambled to retrieve her marbles, placing them protectively under her skirt as if we hadn't noticed them in the first place.

"C'mon, don't be such a Jew, hand them over," instructed the older girl seeking her prize.

I shuddered and glanced around the group. No one batted an eyelid, as at the time, it was common playground language. I happened to be friends with a Jewish girl in class and she got some not-so-friendly ribbing when she took a day off for a Jewish holiday. I'd also become acutely aware that a boy who had a German-sounding name had been punched for no apparent reason. What might people have deduced from my real surname, if only they'd known the full picture? I'd hate to think. I could only conclude that the war and the ratcheting tension had brought out more cruelty in some people.

For days now, I could sense something developing. The teachers in the playground kept noticeably checking the sky. For the umpteenth time, we had to hold up our gas masks in the air to show that we had them with us. We were told with a fake cheerfulness to be ready to follow instructions and to evacuate to the corridor if requested. Still nothing happened.

At the end of the school day, my mother was in an obvious rush and gathered me up quickly to take me home. The news wasn't good. Groups of German planes had bombed the fringes of outer London and others had been spotted skimming overhead in nuisance raids just to trigger the sirens. Mum wanted me home and ready to take cover just in case. With the enemy lurking over the horizon, primed to wreak havoc at a moment's notice, I willed myself into believing that London was exempt from direct attack, as what could be gained from making war on women and children? It surely couldn't happen.

Chapter 6

Predator and Prey

The short and largely happy life I'd known came to an end on September 7, 1940. This was the start of the Blitz, when waves of German bombers darkened the sky over London. It had started like a normal Saturday: clear skies, Mum in the garden and Dad inside the house with his newspaper. Yet come the late afternoon, when the sirens went off, there was no cheery 'all clear' signal to follow. For the first time, columns of slow-moving black dots approached. Etched across the skyline, they looked innocuous and small set against the blue vastness. It was hard to believe that – finally – they had come for us.

Despite months of everyone planning and practising what steps to take if London was bombed, my mind emptied, and I instantly forgot what to do. Caught on the hop, I relied on my parents to grab our gas masks and blankets before I was steered by the small of my back to the bottom of the garden. My two hand-stitched soft toys, Lamby Lumps and Pussy Pieces remained in my grasp, and I called out for our cat, Sandy, even though she was nowhere to be seen.

"C'mon, she's got most of her nine lives left, you've only got the one!" said Dad, as he swept me towards the entrance to the shelter. "She can afford to take her chances outside."

We collectively scrambled out of the light and into the darkness. It was too soon for our eyes to adjust, and we needed to feel our way to the bunk beds. In that first panicky minute, my father groped around trying to start the paraffin lamp in some perverse game of blind-man's buff. Trying his best to appear unperturbed, he kept checking with me that I had my gas mask to hand. Sandwiched uncomfortably next to Mum, I replied "yes" several times until the point came where I doubted myself. Moments later, Dad finally got the lamp lit, illuminating our shelter. On the bunk beside me, I saw my mother's resigned features, whereas my father bore a twisted face, an expression I'd never seen before. And then I spotted an adrenalin-fuelled tremor in his hands. It was little more than twenty years since he'd been groping around inside a bunker and losing the race to find his own gas mask.

In the semi-darkness, we shifted around and sniffed. I could hear my own heavy breathing, whilst taking in the composite stink of the shelter: paraffin, cat wee, body odour and the ever-present linger of cigarettes carried on my parents' clothes. I listened intently, waiting for something to happen, and took my cue from Dad. His chest stopped labouring and was slowing with every breath. Maybe nothing would happen. And then...

Crump-crump-crump.

Although disorientated, I could make out what could only have been distant explosions. I shrunk down into my mattress. My young mind could hardly comprehend what was taking place.

"That's a long way off, not to worry," Dad murmured, as if keeping his voice down might somehow protect us.

"Not to worry" I whispered to Lamby Lumps and Pussy Pieces. I tried to console myself that my father had been under fire before and knew what he was talking about.

Boom-boom-boom.

I jumped at these louder, deeper sounds, which reverberated around the nearby houses and gardens.

"Keep calm," instructed Dad, controlling his voice well. Then he must have seen my confused face. "That's just Big Bertha," he said, "she's one of ours, giving some back."

Nobody had warned me that an anti-aircraft battery had been installed on nearby playing fields. My father, like so many soldiers, gave silly names to military things to make it all seem more bearable. Additional guns quickly joined in, and soon outgoing rounds started to mix with the orchestral whine of falling bombs. Every sound was amplified in the semi-darkness, and I remained keyed up to hear everything possible. Trapped in my own head, I tried to rationalise things: this must be war, then.

We were ill-prepared on that first night as we listened to the metal storm playing out over London while clutching each other during every explosion. Distances were impossible to calculate – we'd get better at that over time. Initially, my mind was occupied thinking about the poor devils being pummelled directly underneath. Somehow, I eventually drifted off to sleep to the boom of outgoing gunfire. If I consider it now, I wonder how I could have possibly slept in those circumstances. I guess I had surrendered to what I didn't know. In the morning, as we emerged unscathed after the first 'all clear' siren, the sky over the East End was noticeably bright and I thought I'd awoken to a particularly beautiful sunrise. That was until my stupidity was pointed out to me.

The commencement of mass air raids on London became a daily battle between predator and prey. For those first few weeks, the raids were nearly always in the daytime, and so school was abandoned as I hunkered down in my troglodyte existence. Ruled by commands from the baying sirens, I soon became mentally exhausted, and each temporary reprieve was marked by me flopping back onto my proper bed. Once awake at some strange, ungodly hour, so began the anxious anticipation of waiting for the bombers to return. For me, the days literally turned upside down. Was I supposed to sleep by day in the shelter and then be awake at nighttime? We learnt that good weather was bad because it brought raids, and really bad weather was good because it didn't. Meanwhile, mixed weather brought 'I don't know' kind of days. So, we crossed our fingers for high winds, filthy cloud and rain. But the weather rarely saved us, and it seemed that almost every day, the lumbering bombers reappeared to do their worst with a grizzly familiarity.

In those early days, listening within the confines of our shelter to the drone of toiling aircraft, we'd sometimes try and guess whether we were hearing friend of foe. That was just wishful thinking on my part, as they were probably always German planes bristling with bombs. We tried to remain hopeful. Did a subtle change in engine pitch mean one of their planes had been hit and would now limp home? In the end, we realised it was just the point where a plane had released the weight of its bombs. Despite the nightly wall of ack-ack being thrown skyward, which at first had stiffened our resolve, I never heard about a bomber crashing down anywhere near us.

As the Blitz intensified, the Germans changed tack and switched to bombing at night. During this most heavy phase, the planes dropped their bombs unsighted through cloud in a more scattergun manner, which meant that across the city, people were being killed in their droves. We weren't living our lives, we were merely existing. Despite this, the newsreels and radio broadcasts continued their upbeat narrative that "London can take it".

Although I sat with Mum and Dad listening to some of these broadcasts, they did a good job of disguising most of the dangers. While I heard my parents talk amongst themselves about who had 'got it' or 'bought it', I hadn't experienced any deaths firsthand in the sense of viewing bodies and limbs strewn in the street. My mum would sometimes tug my hand hard and pull me in the opposite direction if we turned into a road where something was happening. I might hear an ambulance siren or snatch a glance at teams of men picking their way through last night's rubble, but I was initially protected from the very worst and thankful for it.

Indeed, there wasn't the time or space to think too hard about anyone apart from your immediate family. After a night where deep, percussive strikes had ebbed and flowed around us, I'd crawl out from the shelter in the morning feeling glad to be alive. The sky over parts of Central London would be dancing orange from the inferno still raging in the city, and when the docks and warehouses had been hit, it wasn't uncommon to be able to make out the distinctive hint of something like burning sugar, rubber or oil. Always though would be the pervading stench of ruptured gas and raw sewage due to the smashed pipework where nearby streets had been split open.

Even within this chaos, with the daytimes now raid-free, our family quickly adapted, and we got into some sort of routine. As darkness fell, I was expected to change into my nightie and dressing gown and was allowed to fall asleep in my dad's big armchair, my face pressed against the Brylcreem stain circle that he'd left on the material. And when the warning siren went off, he could sometimes take me down to the garden without even waking me. The fact that he could do this shows just how bone-weary I'd already become. If I woke in the night, my mother would be there with kindness and open a precious tin of digestive biscuits. We would munch away slowly, and I'd take little mouse nibbles, like I'd seen my pet mice do, heeding my mother's warning that she didn't know when we might see biscuits again in the shops due to the current sugar shortage. I made sure I got every crumb that had fallen on to my sleeping bag (made from old blankets and my dad's army greatcoat), while listening to the comforting clickety clack of Mum's knitting needles as she worked away nightly crafting jumpers, hats and scarfs by lamplight. After some weeks, I asked her what she was going to do with all these extra items, as she'd produced enough to kit out a small army. "It's for bombed-out families," she explained. "Most of them have only got the clothes they're standing in and not a stick of furniture. It's a disgrace." There was a withering consensus at the time that the government should be doing more to help the victims of the Blitz. All I could offer were my own cast offs.

Over time, we learnt that it wasn't just the enemy's bombs that we had to contend with but the falling shell fragments from our own guns. As my father explained, what goes up must come down, and that included our own anti-aircraft munitions. Sat in our Anderson shelter and subject to the angle of the guns, we'd regularly pick out the offbeat pitter-patter of potentially lethal metal shards dancing off the concrete or nearby roofs, all fired by our own side. Dad listened intently, concerned about the ever-increasing number of damaged or smashed tiles on our roof and how to keep the house watertight. Panes of glass regularly cracked and were hard to replace. It felt like a losing battle.

Every night in our garden shelter, at some point during the evening when he could wait no longer, Dad would venture outside for a smoke. He demonstrated how he could cradle a lit cigarette under his downward-facing palm, like they used to do in their dugouts at Ypres to avoid the snipers. He disclosed this as if he might unintentionally lure down the might of the Luftwaffe upon us. Sometimes, when he crawled back into the shelter, my nose picked up the scent from the slightly scorched flesh of his hand.

I couldn't help myself on those nights and I'd peer outside after him. On occasion, I was presented with the bizarre spectacle of him holding the metal dustbin lid on top of his head for protection against flying shrapnel.

If the bombing wasn't currently nearby and it was absolutely necessary, I was sometimes allowed to run back to the house to use the toilet. I had an aversion to using the outside one in the pitch black, fearing the spiders. Sometimes, though, it was merely an excuse. It was better to be outside for a few moments than cooped up letting my imagination run riot. I recall my first time outside, crunching over the frosted grass to get to the house only to stop in my tracks to gawp upwards, even though I'd promised to be as quick as I could. I felt compelled to point out the planes in the sky, although I was the only soul outside above ground. How beautiful the searchlights looked, I thought. They crisscrossed the sky and occasionally exposed a tiny aircraft, as if they were holding it in place whilst the artillery went pop-pop in the distance. At times, it seemed like there was more traffic in the sky than I ever saw on the roads.

On a rare occasion, when we'd made it back to our bedrooms before first light, we were rudely awoken by the sound of workmen in the banjo. Metal was being collected to help in the war effort. We'd already handed over our aluminium pots and pans at the outbreak of the war, which we were told were needed for aircraft manufacture. Being a young child, I found it quite funny to think that the Spitfires and Hurricanes chasing the Luftwaffe up in the clouds were actually made out of my mum's pans! Now, some new government edict had been passed to requisition all the iron railings and gates.

My father, only half-dressed, went outside to confront the workmen about this latest imposition and to question them over what they intended to take. The material they wanted was wrought iron, but the men with oxyacetylene cutters intended to strip every cast iron gate and railing in sight. It was as if our house was being attacked by our own side.

"You're making a right bugger's muddle of that, it's the wrong bloody stuff," bemoaned my father, knocking on the gate with his knuckles and attempting to shout above the noise. "You need to be up at the posh houses, not here."

But nobody was listening.

Orders were orders, and within an hour or two, the banjo looked naked and unfinished. Years later, after the war, there was anger when piles of unusable cast iron gates and railings were found rusted and stored in an old railway siding, our sacrifice in vain.

Despite the constant threat of air raids and broken sleep, we were forced to get on with life as best we could. This meant Mum had to go shopping nearly every day and hope not to get caught outside in a raid. Like most families, at the start of the war, she'd accumulated lots of store cupboard food such as flour as well as dried things like peas and potatoes, which could be kept in cool places. (Many an Anderson shelter served as an extended larder.) But after a few weeks, once the basics had run out, she had no alternative but to run the risk of heading to town, even though rationing was making that task ever harder. Certain fresh foods, particularly things like bacon, were already scarce. I couldn't be left at home and regularly accompanied Mum, which must have added to her angst. We no longer strolled to the shops like before but rather scuttled, our heads down, like beetles. Simply taking a moment to linger at a shop window was out of the question. Following her lead by hugging the corners and plotting where the next secure point was situated became a matter of potential survival. A public shelter or a strong-looking doorway or an underpass provided a bolthole on our journey in case the Germans returned.

Dad also needed to provide, as there were mounting bills to pay, and he desperately cooked up new schemes that enabled him to make some reasonable money whilst utilising his skills. We didn't have a garden full of chickens and a vegetable plot, and so the additional cash generated helped us to acquire both the basics and occasional extras. He hit on the idea of painting fire screens. These screens, positioned by each coal fire, suddenly became an in-demand safety item because of the Blitz. In a rush to get to a shelter, people couldn't be certain they'd completely extinguished their fires, and so a fire screen acted as a precaution, stopping any remaining hot embers spilling out on to the floor. You wouldn't want to survive a bombing raid only to find that coal fire sparks had set your house on fire.

He teamed up with a friend, who knocked up cheap wooden frames for him, which he could subsequently paint. By keeping his own prices at a sensible level, he could produce an affordable but attractive item for homeowners. Soon, many of our neighbours had a country cottage, alpine view or clipper ship adorning their living room hearth, which brightened up their surroundings during an otherwise miserable time.

There was another memorable event early in the Blitz, when I saw my father rub up against the authorities. One night, during our evening meal, we were startled by a wail outside, which was quickly followed by an urgent knock at our door. My father cursed under his breath as my mother immediately checked the blackout curtains. She'd spent hours carefully decorating them with orange rickrack braid to make them look more cheerful from the inside, and we all assumed that an ARP Warden had spotted a chink of light from the house. That would be a grievous rule breach during the Blitz and could bring a fine. We were used to hearing the mantra, "Put those ruddy lights out", which was expressed in somewhat self-important tones as the evening patrol moved down our street.

Three uniformed men around my father's age, two Local Defence Volunteers and an ARP Warden squeezed into the doorway, flustered and straightening their tin hats. Seeing them in those blue overalls with their shiny buttons and tunic whistles, I feared they wanted to take my father away and make him join the army again, and so I ran to his side. However, it quickly transpired they were local men looking for more volunteers for what was known as 'fire watch duty'. In an inauspicious start to recruiting my father, the ARP Warden had leaned his bike against our front post and hadn't seen Sandy in the pitch dark. All smooth and silky, our cat had slithered a tail across the Warden's face, and he'd yelled out, thinking he'd been assaulted by a ghost.

"We just need one more person to make up the numbers," announced the ARP Warden, composing himself. "Will you join us?" he asked hopefully.

The clock ticked. There was silence. I thought perhaps they just needed to speak up a bit because of my dad's burst eardrum. Then my dad hawked loudly and spat into his handkerchief in one elaborate motion. "I've already done my bit in the last war!" he replied.

Our uninvited guests then tried to explain that *all* the other men in the banjo had agreed to give up their time and were doing their duty, but my dad was having none of it. His face remained a mask of belligerent defiance. Was Dad too thick-skinned to care, or was he just smarter than them?

"I'm not clambering over rooftops like some blue-arsed fly putting out fires with just a stirrup pump," he said. "Find somebody else for your damn fool's errand."

It wasn't that he was afraid – I thought of my dad as a brave man, although all little girls would probably say the same.

I never knew him as left wing, right wing, a violent man or a pacifist. He just wanted to be left alone to paint.

Drawn to the faces of the adults, I swallowed hard, unsure what might happen next. I could tell, as it was so blindingly obvious from my mother's expression, that she felt ashamed and didn't know where to look, although she knew better than to say anything. This was hardly going to help us ingratiate ourselves with the neighbours, who already considered Dad the odd one out. Try as they might, nobody could force Dad or shame him into 'volunteering', and so the standoff ended and they left empty handed.

Once the front door shut, we returned to our supper and sat like statues for a moment. Then, without another word passing between us, we resumed eating. Head down, all I could hear was the slurping of food as we each tried to finish what was on our plate in record time. That confrontation was never mentioned again.

Chapter 7

Scraping By

When a new family unexpectedly moved in next door, I discovered they had relocated from the bombed-out East End. I don't remember our neighbours who had the parrot moving out or where they went, although I clearly recall the big fuss over this new family. They were called the Clements, and there were an awful lot of them for a relatively modest-sized house. There was a youngish man called Fred who had a problem with his legs and wheezed when he spoke. I was temporarily fascinated by his disability and probably said all the wrong things, but he had a self-deprecating sense of humour and didn't seem to mind my inquisitive nature. Then there were two more senior men. One of them, Lionel, I believe was a grandfather. Plus, there was a middle-aged woman only known to me as Mrs Clements, her sister and then, finally, two daughters, Vera and Joyce. They all had brash, cockney accents so thick you could have walked over each sentence. My mum quickly decided they were common and enjoyed living cheek by jowl, and that Lionel clanked because his inner coat pocket was full of ale bottles. Equally, when I told them that Dad was an artist, Mrs Clements rolled her eyes and made a half-formed snorting noise that stuck in her throat. So much for Londoners sticking together!

Given that they'd lost their home, and that Mr Clements was away fighting the war, I thought my mum was being rather mean. I found the two girls particularly interesting. They were probably about the same age as my sister, and to me, they looked like film stars. Vera had very blonde hair (peroxide, my mother scoffed), which was all piled on top like Betty Grable's, and Joyce's red hair was swept up in front with combs. They also appeared to have access to lipstick and painted their fingernails. You could smell them a mile off due to the amount of perfume they wore. The strangest thing to me was that they wiggled their bottoms when they walked.

One early evening, Mrs Clements was waiting for the girls outside, worried they were late back from town with the sirens due to sound at any moment. I must have picked up on her concern and asked where they might be.

"Perhaps they're courtin'" she explained.

"Caught in what?" I asked.

Her face lit up. "'Ark at you," she squawked, falling about laughing. "Ain't you a proper little madam."

After that, Mrs Clements warmed to me considerably.

Vera and Joyce were also good to me, and over time, I increasingly went into their garden to talk to them. It was more mature than ours and had a couple of small apple trees. We'd sometimes gobble up the windfalls, and I'd often help take the brown battered ones down to the pig bin at the end of the road. The girls happily let me pitch in with the dirty work.

They also had a small greenhouse, and as the ruthless bombing progressed, more and more of the glass was shattered, until it became impossible to grow tomato plants. With Mr Clements serving in Egypt, things like that became neglected and fell into disrepair. It was the same in many houses.

I also recall the two girls calling me over to show me some presents their father had sent them all the way from the Middle East. There were three beautiful handbags, one large one for Mrs Clements and two smaller ones for the girls. They were made of pale, soft leather and decorated with camels, pyramids and palm trees. All at once the two girls started crying and I was at a loss to explain why. If my daddy had been abroad and posted me lovely presents, I certainly wouldn't have cried.

*

During the Blitz, we all did our best to scrape by. One day, when he'd finally run out of odd jobs that paid cash in hand, Dad reluctantly agreed to register for war work. As he skulked off into town, his tail between his legs, Mum and I pretended not to see him leave so as not to compound his shame. He was not best pleased when he returned home to tell us the news that his role had been determined by his official listing as an artist.

"Some bright spark with a clipboard has decided it's a good idea that I spray paint aircraft wings for ten hours a day," he moaned.

I had visions of Hurricanes rolling off the production line, each with a bowl of fruit carefully added to the underside.

That first factory job only lasted a few days. After each shift, he'd collapse into an armchair, coughing his lungs up into a hanky due to some sort of allergic reaction to the spray paint. To prove it, he also came out in a spectacular rash, and at the end of his first week, the doctor told him it would kill him if he carried on working there. And so that endeavour came to a swift end, and he was off the hook for a while, waiting for reassignment.

Although Dad might be housebound, I was encouraged to play outside after school so I wouldn't get under his feet. However, my wandering days were curtailed and I had to remain close to the house so that in the event of a raid, Mum could call me in at a moment's notice. She needn't have worried as my hunger usually propelled me home at teatime – I had no need for a wristwatch. When I couldn't stand it any longer, I burst indoors ravenous, hoping for something different or special, but usually it was just bread with something like condensed milk to spread on top.

Like most Londoners, the ongoing rationing meant our diets had narrowed and become ever more basic and repetitive. In turn, bowel movements (or a lack of them) were a regular topic of conversation and a whole industry developed to tackle these problems. Opening any magazine or newspaper of the day, you would surely find adverts for pills, potions and tonics. Once a week, I was made to drink a glass of what was called Parrish's Food, which was a sort of liquid syrup that you might feed to house plants today. It looked and tasted rather like a glass of blood, although I was assured it was full of iron and would keep me fit and strong. Sometimes, I was given a small piece of Ex-Lax, designed to work 'downstairs' to speed things up. Whilst it

VALERIE BRAUNSTON – LONDON CAN TAKE IT

looked a lot like chocolate and tasted a little bitter, it retained enough of a chocolate-like quality to mean I was more than happy to munch on what had been handed to me.

Whilst my primary objective was to avoid being bombed, I decided that mere survival wasn't enough and so I developed a keen interest in finding nice things to eat. By nice, I mean sweet. With pocket money in hand, I was sometimes allowed to go to the local shops on Saturday mornings to see what I could buy, although there was already precious little choice. Pear Drops, Lemon Sherbets and Dolly Mixtures were still on the shelves in big jars and sold by weight, and I watched with a sinking heart as supplies dwindled lower each week. I desired anything sweet, and if there weren't any other options, I'd sometimes be reduced to Ovaltine tablets or cough sweets, as they weren't on the ration. Occasionally, I was able to find Lyons fruit pies or slices that tasted like carboard; heaven knows what gloopy substance masqueraded as the filling. At one time, a rumour circulated that the chocolate dispensing machines at our railway station had been filled by a benefactor for a troop of boy scouts on a day trip. Of course, they had all gone by the time I got there – either that or they had never existed in the first place. That didn't stop me regularly swinging by just to check. What did appear at the train station one day was known as a 'name tape machine'. This allowed you, for a few coins, to manipulate a dial and stamp letters and numbers onto a thin metal strip. I think the machine might have been for labelling suitcases, but it became a craze among the local children to create their own dog tags. We'd seen so many parents and relatives in uniform with them that it became desirable to have a set of your own. When my parents challenged me as to why I'd wasted my weekly pocket money

72

on producing my own name strip, they shook their heads when I replied fatalistically that it would help people identify me if I was pulled out from under a wrecked house.

During this period, I learnt the key to having a full stomach was acquiring first-rate information whilst side-stepping unhelpful rumours, and I was grown up enough to actively assist my mother. When I spied a boy shooting past us in the street on his bicycle, something about the determined look on his face and the speed at which he was going gave him away. I nudged Mum and the pair of us scampered down the road in the direction that he'd just come from with high expectation and an empty shopping bag. Only a few hundred feet down Main Avenue, we were rewarded with the site of a parked van outside Ashtons the grocer's shop. What had they brought today? We spotted onions in nets and various tinned items being carried into the shop's side entrance. Other women hurriedly formed a queue, determined not to miss out, and within minutes, a snaking line had developed out of the ether. Whilst I waited, my wandering eyes took in the messy street. At best, a few dislodged tiles here and there had slid down roofs, reminding me of a card trick gone wrong. In places, demolition gangs had pulled down some of the houses, leaving telling gaps; it was as if a great giant had trampled the land.

We took our turn and stepped into the shop in high anticipation. As I stood with my mother and she exchanged her coupons for rationed items, I heard her ask, "Have you got anything under the counter?" She tried a charming smile and pushed me forward to be in plain view. In the early days, we'd benefited on more than one occasion from an extra piece of chicken or some more tea, as a sympathetic shopkeeper patted me on the head. Now, though, each transaction took place under the scrutiny of the row of women behind, who were watching like hawks for any signs of rule bending. Latterly, the only treat I might sometimes receive from a shopkeeper was something called 'Spanish wood', which I could suck and chew. It had a sweet, liquorice flavour.

*

We learnt that the only way not to lose heart and drift into self-pity was to make the most of any small pleasures. Throughout the Blitz, we did things as a family to keep our spirits up, including regular trips to the cinema. Despite the government's question 'Is Your Journey Necessary?', the picture houses, as we commonly referred to them, were always buzzing. For a handful of coins, Hollywood transported me to incredible, colourful places, whether that was the Wild West or a city of skyscrapers. To spend a few hours away from our narrow, threatened lives was the very definition of escapism, and before any American troops had set foot on our soil, I'd already been indoctrinated into believing their homeland was a place of wonder.

We had three picture houses just up the road in Enfield Town – the Savoy, the Rialto and the rather exotically named Florida. This last one was actually a bit of a fleapit, and the Savoy was the grandest, with Doric columns, fake marble and huge red velvet curtains. Each cinema had one large screen with seats that could easily take over a thousand paying customers.

People were desperate to see the new releases and so there were always queues, and my dad would often rush ahead to secure our place. Unfortunately, the quality of the films and projectors was quite poor back then and the sound could be erratic. I remember asking my parents (because of the grainy picture) why it always rained in every film, even during the indoor scenes. It was not uncommon for the projector to break down part way through the film, which would invoke jeers and catcalls from the cheaper seats. It was all part of the experience, and we took it in our stride.

At the Rialto, there would sometimes be an organist who rose up from the floor below in the most dramatic manner, and we were always encouraged to sing along with the words on the screen. I'm not sure if this was planned or to help cover up sound quality issues. During the war, it didn't take much to create a bit of a sing-song, and that collective act, in the cinema or in the pub, was one of the few ways open to people to keep their chins up, particularly during tough times.

My favourite of the three was the Rialto because it boasted an ornamental pond in the foyer, complete with goldfish. Often, whilst Dad lined up for the tickets, he'd suggest I kneel and look at the fish (even though I could see them perfectly well standing up). I later realised that he used this little trick to get me into films that were too old for me. *Gone with the Wind* stands out in my memory, even though some of the themes were quite adult for my young mind. I lapped it up anyway. When we got home, to my mother's chagrin and my dad's amusement, I stood on a chair in my nightie and became Scarlet O'Hara – "I'll never be hungry again," I declared in a southern accent only slightly worse than Vivienne Leigh's.

In those days, we'd often see two films in a row. Sometimes, there would be a cartoon in the middle, plus a government newsreel that kept us up to date with what was happening in the war. These were shown on repeat, so it didn't really matter what time you arrived, as you could camp there all day if you wanted. I watched the news with interest, as unlike listening to it on the radio, I could look at images of the far-off places being talked about. However, I got a sense that it wasn't just my father who was rather disbelieving of some of what we were being told. An odd groan or laugh in the wrong place suggested many adults in the audience believed they were being shown propaganda.

If there was an air raid, the information was flashed up on screen and we were given the option of leaving for a public shelter, although the film would always continue and the vast majority remained in their seats, with people unwilling to take their chances outside. We always sat tight, as the solid walls of a cinema felt a lot more impregnable than being interred in a tomb-like Anderson shelter. That was until the beautiful Alcazar picture house in Edmonton took a direct hit and was completely destroyed. After that, nowhere felt safe.

On one late afternoon outing, as we turned on to the High Street, we walked back to our bus stop with a near neighbour called Ken, who was on leave from the RAF and had also been at the same picture house. I remember looking at him proudly, as he was smart and handsome in his uniform, only having that warm feeling dashed as he flinched at the sound of some distant bombs detonating over London. Evening was nearly upon us. I recall that he had a rather horrified stare on his face as he looked up at the reddening sky.

"I don't know how you can stand that n-night after night," he stammered to my parents. "I'll be glad when my leave is over as I feel safer up there in a plane."

*

After so many nights sleeping in the garden, my father decided it would do me some good to get out of the house, and so, on a crisp, bright day, I excitedly put on my knitted gloves in expectation, not knowing what my dad had in store for us. My father-daughter trip turned out to be a visit to the ack-ack (or anti-aircraft) battery just off Southbury Road and wasn't quite what I'd had in mind. This particular battery was attached to a small, hastily built camp, which was a set of wooden billets surrounding a parade ground. There was a flagpole in the middle, where a limp Union Jack had been hoisted. We sat on the side of the road opposite the main entrance with the sandwiches Mum had packed us and, of course, our trusty gas masks by our sides. Behind stretched reels of barbed wire, we watched the artillerymen huffing and puffing to move large shells into neat piles next to each gun in readiness for the coming night. Dad came across as moderately interested in what they were doing, or perhaps his mind was drifting back in time. To me, it looked very similar to the local publican receiving barrels of beer off the brewer's dray outside the Rose and Crown.

We made small talk whilst we ate our sandwiches. Earlier, I'd thought of lots of important questions to ask my dad once I had him all to myself, but when the time came, for once, my mind went blank. Dad somehow had this knack of letting you know that silence was also fine. If only my teachers had learnt the same trick! We sat and studied the goings on and then Dad slipped a small bag of marbles into my gloved hand. He must have found a shop that still had some stock. Affection was another thing strictly rationed with my father and I have no childhood recollection of ever being kissed or cuddled by him, as that was how things were. However, he tried to make up for it in his own small ways, and what young girl wouldn't relish the simple pleasure of a bag of marbles from her daddy?

Chapter 8
Missing Fingers

During the winter months of the Blitz, London continued to attract German bombers like a magnet, although other large cities had begun taking their turn in the firing line. The most devastating attack was against Coventry, and when we saw the pictures of their city centre and the gutted cathedral, it appeared to have been wiped off the map.

I never got any respite though, as London wasn't spared for more than a day or two at best. During one particularly harrowing raid over a two-night period, just as I was looking forward to New Year, the incendiaries and high explosives overwhelmed our firemen and whole swathes of the city went up in flames. It became known as 'The Second Great Fire of London'. During that period of carnage, the idea of a blackout became ludicrous as you could've surely spotted London from the moon. That night, Dad could smoke outside in the garden with impunity and was shocked that it was bright enough to read a newspaper!

We didn't want to become another Coventry, and everyone demanded to know where our protection was. Further up the road on Bullsmoor Lane, a great, noisy battery of four extra anti-aircraft guns was hauled into position to defend that end of Enfield. As the attacks in our neck of the woods intensified, had the addition of these guns surreptitiously raised the stakes? The neighbourhood started to speculate that any concentration of artillery acted like a lightning rod, a clear giveaway that there was something worth defending.

From the outbreak of the war, I'd picked up a sense of local pride that just north of us were the factories that had made the famous Lee-Enfield rifle, the standard issue British-made gun of the First World War. Dad would point them out to me whenever the Home Guard paraded. Now those same factories were once again churning out vital new weapons for the war effort, and many local men worked there. Anyone with a modicum of sense knew that these buildings and surrounding warehouses would fall victim to the bomber's inexorable demand for new targets. What we perhaps didn't realise was that, like the River Thames, the Lee Valley waterway and reservoirs running parallel to the Great Cambridge Road provided a useful navigational aid for the bombers, as the moonlight could be seen reflecting off them. With the military expansion all around us, it finally dawned on my parents that we weren't living in such an advantageous location after all.

When a nearby school in Edmonton was hit by a large bomb, the authorities feared that such block buildings resembled a factory from above, and so my school was temporarily shut again. (It re-opened only days later, presumably because children left to wander the streets or parents staying away from work to mind them caused a different set of issues.) At this point, I started to notice the incessant adult gossip about why certain important buildings had been hit, why others hadn't received so much as a scratch and the best way to avoid getting killed. A certain paranoia crept in, as people worried that spies might be signalling the bombers at night with lanterns. It made everyone suspicious of their neighbours or newcomers. Idle minds with little else to do also took a deep interest in newspaper horoscopes, which grew in popularity, as if one might find their fate printed there in black and white.

Whilst we remained in the thick of it, Mum continued to act as a calming influence, ensuring I was awake, washed and fed before walking me the short distance to school. When it got dark and the sirens sounded once again, she always made time to tell me with her best half-smile that everything would be fine. That was until one time when Dad was in earshot and added the proviso "unless it's a 'smackeroo'"– his word for a direct hit. Mum glared at him for not keeping his mouth shut. If looks could kill.

I don't quite recall when, but as the mercury plummeted in the depths of winter, there was a point where we stopped rushing to the garden shelter at the first wail of the siren. Some might call it foolishness; others might use the term resilience. My parents would wait, listening for the tell-tale sounds of the bomb blasts or, in contrast, the silence that might suggest a false alarm. If it was the docks and the East End getting hit again, we took a chance and hid in the large cloakroom under the stairs for warmth and extra protection. Dad put a blackboard over the lavatory seat to provide additional seating, and we all crammed inside like mackerel in a tin.

The problem was that in a sitting position, sleep was out of the question. A quiet indoor pursuit, well suited for a small girl to while away the hours when sheltering, was wool gathering.

This involved me collecting fluff from carpets, coats and jumpers from around the house in advance of the expected raid. Once we were in our hiding place, I would press the wool into a shoebox lid to make an attractive pattern. My parents never suspected that I was regularly gleaning material from Pam's favourite camel-haired coat, and my sister would have skinned me alive if she'd ever found out. Sometimes, we played card games, which were a good way to pass the time. I also liked to play I spy, although given the small space we were confined to, my parents must have found this excruciatingly dull.

My mother used her time as productively as possible. The newspapers and wireless kept encouraging us to 'make do and mend', but we didn't need to be told – self-preservation gave us little choice. At this point, we couldn't afford to waste anything, and every item had a second use, often achieved with great ingenuity and humour, as we felt we were doing something positive to outwit Hitler. For instance, my mother would regularly mend clothes or unravel a worn jumper and then wash and hang the wool in the vain hope that all the kinks would eventually fall out. Having divided the wool into skeins, my small hands would be put to good use when we took ourselves off to the cloakroom again, when she'd make me stretch out my arms to use for winding the wool around. I would complain impatiently, asking to play I spy one more time. When dry, she would miraculously transform the wool into pixie hoods for me, and sometimes a crochet hat to send to Pam.

Was it rash to skip hiding in our outside Anderson shelter? In the harshest winter period, the shelter was open to the elements and was cold, damp and claustrophobic, with no heating, cooking facilities or a toilet. It really was just a corrugated roof with a few inches of soil on top. Our exposed and solitary existence was quite different to the newsreel images we'd see at the pictures, where Londoners crowded together deep down and secure in various tube stations, benefiting from their natural warmth. That gave a false impression – it wasn't how most of us living away from the big stations got by.

However, there were still many nights when the bombs dropped around us, and we had no choice but to return to the shelter. We added little creature comforts such as a Thermos for hot drinks, and my mother also used to fill milk bottles with near-boiling water, so we could cradle them like hot water bottles, careful not to knock them over ourselves or the wooden boards. Huddled together in our homemade woollies and our underwear in tatters, we somehow survived in our draughty shelter. In all the streets around us, we knew that everyone was in the same boat.

At first light, with the bombers gone and the sweet sound of the 'all clear' once again, we would dust ourselves down and leave the sour, frigid air of the shelter behind us. I got into the habit of assisting my parents with the regular task of checking over the house to ensure it was still intact. Once, I discovered my goldfish on the floor, still alive but flopping around and gasping for air in a small pool of water. They must have thrown themselves out of their glass tank due to a nearby bomb detonation. It was a close shave, and I was glad to be able to save them. I could breathe more easily once I knew everything was still standing, with my bedroom untouched. Then, with the survival of another raid under my belt, I'd quickly get permission to commence my search for any nearby shrapnel. My parents would usually agree, so long as it wouldn't make me late for school. Marbles could no longer compete with what we considered free toys from above, not dissimilar to conkers. It was quickly understood that some items had greater collectability than others. At first, any bit of metal had value, but items that largely kept their identifiable shape became the most coveted at my school, such as the tail fins from incendiaries or the conical precision steel warheads from our own guns that turned a hint of blue after being fired. Once I got my eye in, I could sometimes find these distinctive shapes within the general scattering of tortured metal pieces.

The weeks continued to pass, and the weather began to brighten as we approached Easter 1941 and our seventh month under attack. Like so many schoolchildren, I yawned throughout the day and occasionally found myself yanked alert by a sound or motion that might mean the start of another raid. Perhaps being so exhausted helped deaden me to the experience. Yet it was hard not to notice the missing children, which was brought home during morning registration.

"Has anyone seen Isabel Matthews?" asked the teacher, scanning our faces.

"She won't be coming to school again," someone piped up.

"Has she moved away, or...?"

I'd already heard the news first thing, but I was too afraid to speak up.

From the back of the class came the gut-wrenching reply. "No, Miss, their house came down on top of them last night."

The teacher's hand hovered over the register for a moment and then she continued. There was no time to dwell, no choice but to move on. The new children started twitching as they looked around the class. They had moved to our part of London and been told they'd be fine here. Now they realised the lie.

Another vivid memory from that time was seeing a young boy wearing a different school uniform paraded in front of the school. We were informed he was from the Tottenham area, and he looked a bit snivelly, with fresh cut marks running up his face. It was clear he really didn't want to be there, particularly when a teacher on the low stage pulled up his arm to reveal a freshly bandaged hand with what looked like some missing fingers. There followed a big speech warning those assembled about how dangerous and stupid it was to go near or pick up unexploded munitions. Of particular concern were the small, hand-sized incendiary devices that were scattered in the thousands every night by our airborne arsonist friends, designed to punch through roofs and set fire to people's lofts. Many of these fell in trees and bushes, with some not going off at all while others were on timer fuses. Buckets of sand were dotted around the school, which we were meant to throw over anything that dropped near us. It was hardly sophisticated.

After so many months of suffering, the Blitz had created bands of feral children, usually boys, who snuck out at night and formed little gangs with the aim to follow the ARP and Fire Wardens to precisely where the incendiaries had fallen. It was all the talk of the playground. Collecting shrapnel was one thing, but some of the naughtiest boys would take the heads off the incendiary devices, tip out the magnesium and then set the contents alight in buckets. Every night could be Bonfire Night.

We'd been warned many times about such things, and I suppose the school was trying to use shock tactics to make their point. I was still quite young, and I was disturbed by the image of the bandaged boy being manhandled off the stage, presumably to repeat the same exercise at the next school. I couldn't fathom why some boys would choose to be outside during an active raid or to set off explosives. However, as we made our way back to class, the boys behind me whispered excitedly to each other, and I heard one of them say, "Well, it's only a couple of fingers!"

Despite all these hardships, in an odd way, there were moments when I enjoyed the extra time the Blitz afforded me to cosy up to my parents and get extra attention. A particular shared intimacy was reading the letters we received, which my parents often reserved for the shelter. Pam wrote regularly, and we enjoyed her correspondence because she sounded so happy, and there was no talk of bombs. My mother used to read them out whilst Dad nodded his head with approval. We usually constructed a swift reply, all chipping in with stories and views, although we never directly mentioned the Blitz.

One day, we had a parcel with a note inside from Uncle Phil from Canada, which was a rare yet welcome event. Suspecting there would be goodies inside, my instinct was to tear into the wrapping paper, but Mum took over, and I noticed how carefully she undid the string and paper. These were now prized items in themselves that could be used again. Our exposure to the never-ending Blitz had taught us that no one was coming to our aid and we had to be self-reliant.

Inside the parcel were some precious tins of fruit and other luxuries that had me licking my lips. Mum opened the letter from Phil conveying that he was sorry to hear about all the raids in London, which continued to make the headlines at home. He hinted that we should consider escaping the worst of it and joining him in Canada. In an age when foreign travel was almost unheard of, if my parents ever discussed it as an option, it didn't happen in front of me. Besides, the German submarine wolf packs were sinking ships at will, and so any such journey would have meant dicing with death.

When my mother and I headed to the post office the next day, I saw firsthand several damaged properties. The fronts of several houses had slid away and were now rubble in the street. I can only describe them as looking like dolls houses, where the hinged door had been opened to reveal everything inside, with the curtains flapping away in the breeze. Whilst my mother sighed and said, "those poor, poor families", I couldn't wrench my eyes away, grimly absorbed and not fully recognising the human tragedy. It was only when I gazed on someone's inner bedroom and toilet that I averted my gaze, as it seemed rude to stare at such things. I crossed my fingers and hoped our luck would hold out.

At the post office, Mum gave me the letter to hold for Uncle Phil whilst she asked the postmistress whether items being sent to Canada would still get there. I couldn't help but notice that in yet another version of the family name, the envelope was quite clearly addressed to Phil Brownston rather than Braunston or Braunstein.

*

Now nearing its eighth consecutive month, the relentless Blitz continued to grind us down. We suffered plenty of near misses, and I admit there were times when I might have been close to breaking point. But what happens when you go beyond breaking point? We couldn't abandon our home, and there was always the hope that at some point this would all end... surely it had to end? And so, we continued to endure.

One evening, something described to me as a 'landmine bomb' exploded near our estate. We very much feared these powerful floating bombs on parachutes that could take out swathes of houses at rooftop height. We got away with that one. And when a high explosive bomb smashed deep into the ground a couple of streets away, whilst the houses in the banjo remained intact, for some reason, the reverberation cracked everyone's outside toilet bowls. The next day, all the broken white bowls were placed on the kerb opposite each house ready for civil collection. I thought they looked like a giant set of false teeth.

At this point in the war, my health started to go downhill. I'd recently suffered in quick succession a bout of chicken pox and then mumps. Many children also started to catch various nasty skin conditions. Scabies was doing the rounds, and whilst I avoided the indignity of being scrubbed down with foul-smelling chemicals, I suffered from boils, due no doubt to our limited diets and cramped conditions. My teacher told me I wasn't getting enough variety of fruit, and I thought how much I'd welcome an orange. I hadn't had one in a long time, as they were reserved for the under-fives and pregnant women, although I'd heard that most of our oranges were probably at the bottom of the sea, courtesy of the U-boat scourge. Mum commented scathingly that it would be more useful if my teacher provided me with some fruit rather than offering her homespun diagnosis.

Other more menacing illnesses swirled around London's schools, as half-fed, dishevelled children intermingled. Schools must have been a breeding ground for disease. I was only a baby when Pam suffered a bout of diphtheria, which was still talked about as 'a bit touch and go'. Back then, Mum used to take it in turns with another mother to escort their two little girls to school each day, insisting they held hands as they went. When the other girl contracted diphtheria, she sadly didn't make it, and I can't imagine the agony my parents went through waiting to see if Pam would succumb as well.

In the end, I developed five boils the size of golf balls on the soft inside skin of my thighs. My mother tried to draw them out by bathing them in scalding hot water that was so unbearable I would plead with her to stop.

"Pleeease, Mum."

"There's no choice, you have to put on a brave face."

At least it got me off running at school for a few days.

The issue of my boils masked something more serious. I recall some days of feeling a bit peaky, and I even started going off my food. The illness was hard to pin down before I lapsed into bouts of fever. As we camped in our shelter and a bomber flew directly overhead, I have memories of a stick of bombs exploding one after the other, creeping ever nearer. I was wrapped in multiple blankets and still burning up. It was an odd sensation because even though the ribs of our shelter started to creak and groan as the bombs fell nearby, I felt strangely accepting and barely flinched. As the detonations passed directly overhead in a series of deafening thumps, my mother threw herself on top of me in an instinctive act. It must have been that close.

Whilst the bombs had missed us this time, straddling the nearby streets instead, Mum was left crying, having inadvertently impaled herself on one of her knitting needles. My father struggled in the close confines and poor light of the shelter to assist whilst she angrily pushed him away. "How am I meant to carry a small child with a raging temperature into a hole in the ground?" she demanded to know.

I tried to say I was alright and wanted them to stop fighting. I'm not sure if the words ever came out. At some point, I must have slipped into a semi-delirious state. Little did I know that I had become extremely ill.

Chapter 9
Yellow Jaundice

The next thing I remember is being propped up in bed. It was daytime and the curtains had been pulled open. I squinted hard as the light poured through. The reassuring presence of my parents lifted my spirits.

"How do you feel?" asked Mum in soft tones. "We tried to get you to a hospital."

"Out of the question," explained Dad. "Full to capacity with casualties from those last raids."

"How long till I need to go back to the shelter?" I asked weakly, my mind still attuned to the nightly routine. I wasn't sure if I could manage it.

With palpable relief, my parents informed me there hadn't been any raids over the entire country for several nights now. Could it really be that the bombing was over? On some level, I understood that we might have been through the worst of it, although given my state, that was hard to take in.

Not long after, a doctor came by the house, and once upstairs, he lent forward to inspect me closely. This immediately registered in me a certain seriousness. Keeping ourselves healthy was a priority because doctors were a scarce resource, although if you did need one, home visits were the norm and nothing to do with the war. Our regular doctor, Dr Harker, was also known to us as Hurricane Harker on account of his tendency to start writing out a prescription before you'd had time to explain what your symptoms were. I was fortunate this morning because it was his partner, Dr Lester, who'd come to see me. He was amiable and sat at the end of my bed making small talk with my parents about the war whilst waiting for the thermometer to register. From their conversation, I could tell he'd been here previously, when I must have been out for the count.

He shined a small light into my watery eyes whilst murmuring to himself until he declared that I was on the mend.

"Two arms, two legs, no need to worry the hospital, little lady," he joked.

Poor Dr Lester was well-liked by our family and, I believe, especially fond of me. His own young daughter had tragically died of polio (or infantile paralysis as it was known then). In a twist of fate, she'd been sent to relatives in America to escape the war and had caught it just days after arriving.

Holding up a small hand mirror, I was allowed to see my curious, olive-coloured skin before Dr Lester confirmed to my parents that he thought I'd been suffering from a serious form of yellow jaundice. The doctor then had a no-nonsense conversation with Mum about what things to give me and, as he rattled off a list of foods, she began screwing up her face at the prospect of this challenge. As many varieties of meat, fruit and vegetables as possible was the answer, plus lots of Bovril. I was just glad not to hear the words 'raw liver sandwiches' on the doctor's list. The other instruction was to increase my levels of fluids, as I'd probably been badly dehydrated. In recent weeks, I'd been encouraged to go into the shelter as 'dry' as possible each night, to reduce my need to go to the toilet. Once in our shelter, that meant either the indignity of peeing in a potty in front of my parents – not an enjoyable experience for anyone – or leaving the relative protection of the shelter to put myself in harm's way.

I remember letting my head return to the pillow, still bouncing the words 'yellow jaundice' around my mind and feeling rather satisfied – it sounded survivable and a little bit special.

Apart from being unable to get up, the other reason I knew I was seriously ill was because when the room began to empty, my father re-entered and sat on the edge of my bed with a large cigar box in his hands. For reasons only known to Dad, he kept a collection of World War One souvenirs that only came down from a top shelf to be shared on *very* special occasions. Normally, this shoebox-sized wooden container resided high up and out of reach from my grasp. No one was permitted to touch it.

Allowing me to open the box, I drew in the distinctive rich aroma, which was never disappointing. To cling on to the smell a moment longer, I even learnt to press a thumbnail into the soft interior wood. I took the weight of each object in my palms and can still recall every item today. For my young self, the shiny items stood out the most: his two war service medals with their colourful ribbons and his name etched along the edge. Then there were three spent rifle cartridges that must have once been a golden brass colour but had dulled a little from handling. Then there was a small, silver crucifix that he told me he'd taken from a dead German alongside a trench map with some scribbled notes that he'd made when his platoon had gone 'over the top' at Passchendaele. Finally, there were two unspent bullets that I needed to handle carefully. One of them had a small notch carved into the tip. My father sat on the bed and pointed it out, explaining to me that when he was in the war, soldiers made these cuts with their knives to turn the bullets into dumdums. I had no idea what that meant but these seemed like important additional facts, and I promised myself I'd try and remember them, even though my head was starting to ache, and I probably needed more sleep.

I never understood then and still don't today exactly why my dad had accumulated this hotchpotch collection of items, or quite what each meant to him and why a father and his little girl could turn the items over in their hands and find them quite so enthralling. How was it possible for my father to try and forget the last war as well as keep those memories alive, all at the same time?

Dad took the bullets back first as he packed his things away and carefully closed the lid. I recognised that keeping two live bullets in a house with children wasn't a particularly sensible thing to do. When I mentioned this, he deflected with a shrug, telling me, "One of my pals still has a live Mills bomb in his house, brought back from France, which he uses as a paperweight."

I thought how you wouldn't want to knock on his front door at the wrong time to demand he does fire watch duty!

My next request was whether he'd let me squeeze my growing collection of shrapnel into the cigar box. I'd already acquired dozens of pieces and outgrown Mum's mangle drawer, where they presently resided. He thought about it for a while and eventually replied no, although he did promise to furnish me with a special box solely for my own material. I drifted off to sleep again feeling rather content.

When the doctor arrived for a further visit, I must have been much improved because he spent more time outside in the hallway with my father than he did with me. It subsequently transpired that the doctor had taken a shine to one of his original paintings on the wall, which my father was more than happy to sell to him. Every doctor's visit and any prescriptions had to be paid for at the time, and so my father would have been delighted to come away from the exchange with cash in his pocket. I picked up the sound of the painting being taken down and the doctor leaving, followed shortly by an argument brewing all the way down from the kitchen. I heard my mother furiously slamming vegetables on to her wooden board and her knife chopping away at machine-gun speed.

"I'll paint you another one, you'll never miss it," Dad remonstrated. "What do you want in its place, a Spanish galleon, a bowl of anemones? Take your pick, you can have whatever you like."

By the time I was well enough to be up and dressed, there hadn't been any raids for a week or so, and it was considered that the Germans had seen sense after their mounting losses. This phase of the war had thankfully come to an end, although it wasn't a conclusive end as we didn't know what might come next. I was just relieved that we were no longer using the Anderson shelter. Sandy sought my attention and many other surviving cats from our area became more visible, though dogs had become a rare commodity. Many went demented during the Blitz, constantly howling and whining, which led their owners to dispose of them. Fortunately, Sandy remained unphased by events and in one piece, although that 'piece' had got bigger. While the remaining cats in the neighbourhood looked scraggier than ever, Sandy had developed a noticeably protruding tummy. It never dawned on me what the obvious explanation might be. (Many years after the war, my mother confessed that Sandy had produced kittens, and she'd ordered Dad behind my back to get rid of them. He'd drowned them in a bucket of water in the back garden. Even today, I still feel heartbroken for those poor kittens that I never even met. I struggle to imagine my parents collaborating over such a grievous act, although I don't know what else could have been done and it does show how hard life was during the war.)

As I slowly continued my recovery, I filled in my time by painting, and it soon became apparent that I'd inherited some of my father's talent. I could feel it within me. Suddenly, I started to use every available piece of paper that I could lay my hands on. My mother watched with mild amusement, proud of my efforts but no doubt thinking that one artist in the family was quite enough. Mum always insisted that she wasn't artistic and shared that as a child, she'd washed the drawings off her school slate with the tears from her eyes. I didn't agree and knew she was creative in so many other ways.

When I learnt that adult books often came with a few plain pages at the front and back, I began hunting around the house armed with a pair of scissors to snip them out for my exclusive use. To Pam, a book was something rather sacred, and so she would have considered this act as desecration.

I kept a precious set of coloured pencils in a tin, which Dad patiently sharpened with his pocket penknife. Felt tip pens hadn't yet been invented, and I think I would have died of happiness if such a thing had been presented to me. To try and get the maximum use out of each pencil, Dad would whittle away at the ends, stroke by stroke, until eventually they were too short to handle, even for my slight fingers.

My father liked to pass this time with me talking about the various locations he used for his inspiration, particularly the places in England he'd visited. He told me about one of his favourite destinations – Alum Bay and The Needles rocks on the Isle of Wight. He'd tell me how dramatic the sea was there, and how the light was excellent for painting. He promised me that when the war was over, we would visit on a family holiday. I didn't really understand what a family holiday was or if I'd been on one before. The closest thing I could recall to such a trip was visiting Virginia Water in Surrey, where I paddled and pretended to be at the seaside.

With my enthusiasm building, I wanted to understand why we couldn't go there now.

"The whole south coast is out of bounds," Dad explained. "Hitler's lot are only spitting distance away on the other side of the channel. Pull a sketch pad out of your pocket and you'd likely be arrested at the point of a bayonet as a spy."

I fell in love with the idea of the Isle of Wight and all the small details of how we would take a train with our suitcases down to the south coast before boarding a steam ferry to cross the Solent. Dad described the island from memory, with its fine beaches and sun-baked sand, where you could sit all day and buy ice creams. Of course, when we went, nothing would be rationed. It all sounded so idyllic.

My parents wanted to travel to Norfolk to collect Pam, and with so much of the transport system wrecked, that meant an overnight trip. It would be easier all round if I went to stay with Auntie Vi, my dad's sister, for a couple of weeks while I continued to recuperate.

Mum tried to tidy my hair up a bit. "A change of scenery will do you some good and your aunt will probably spoil you rotten," she said.

I didn't need much persuasion as my fuzzy memory of Auntie Vi was that she was quite wealthy. Dad frowned, adding, "Don't get too used to it."

It was the first time since the bombing that I'd travelled outside my local vicinity. Mum was apprehensive at the train station, unsure what was reliably running or how long the journey might take. She had to haul my case up every step as I couldn't assist. My strength wasn't quite there yet.

I'd be lying if I told you the route we took and the places we passed through, but what I can say with certainty is that at times, the level of destruction was far greater than anything I'd observed before. Every gap told a story of lives violently interrupted. Although spring had well and truly arrived, I saw bomb-blasted roads that had bare gardens and leafless trees and appeared trapped in a permanent state of winter. I was shocked into silence, knowing few people could have survived there.

It took several hours to pick our way across a pockmarked London, and I was extremely tired by the time we got to Raynes Park. However, I considered the journey ever so worthwhile because the first impression of my temporary new home was that I'd arrived at some sort of oasis. My aunt and uncle had a wonderful property with a half-acre garden that included their own tennis court, a large lily pond with a bridge and a swing chair with a canopy that I soon made full use of. It was like some form of paradise to a girl who had just spent the best part of eight months under siege with a corrugated roof for a ceiling.

Like Dad, my Auntie Vi was in her forties, and she was happily married to a wealthy businessman, whom I called Uncle Douglas. Despite the war, they could only be described as enjoying a good life, yet I bore them no grudges. To me, their lifestyle indicated better times ahead. Uncle Douglas was a short man with a wig who wouldn't go out without his hat on to keep everything in place. I was informed that he was well bred. He also suffered from traces of a stutter, which my dad had been at great pains to point out was "a weakness of character" and nothing inherited from the Great War, because he hadn't served. I didn't care because he was warm and kind to me. I spent many happy hours in my auntie and uncle's garden making imaginary meals for my toys from the fallen seeds and fruit. For those first days, it was as if I could live my pre-war childhood all over again. This enchanted Auntie Vi, who revealed that she wished I was her little girl.

There was also a magnificent mulberry tree, and I remember being fascinated with the mounds of distinctly purple poo from all the birds that fed from it. I'd never seen anything like it.

Uncle Douglas told me that every year, they sold the leaves for silk manufacturing because it was the silkworms' favourite food, which was just the sort of anecdote that a nature-mad girl like me devoured. Auntie Vi couldn't bear creepy crawlies, so she spent little time in her large garden and employed somebody part-time to take care of it. I remember how even the frogspawn in her pond made her nervous, because when she needed some mint picking, she got me to do the honours.

My first Sunday morning with them came as a bit of a shock, as I was expected to dress up and attend church. Auntie Vi read my face and was rather disapproving on the subject, saying that I'd grown up in a godless house and she would need to buy me something more suitable to wear for the following week. The war changed people in so many ways, and the church we attended in Raynes Park was full to the brim. Most of our teachers had also tried to drum it into us that we must go to church and behave well to keep God on our side. I could hear my dad's voice in my head saying, "What we really need is the Americans on our side."

My father was not alone in turning his back on religion. I don't know if he'd ever been much of a believer, but he was always quick to say, "After all the things I've seen..." before leaving the sentence to hang in the air. I suspect Mum viewed things differently, although Dad always had the last word, and I was happy to sit on the fence.

Auntie Vi and Uncle Douglas didn't have any children of their own and so particularly enjoyed spoiling me and taking me to the shops. I was more than happy to oblige. I thought it was a real shame they hadn't become parents, because I only ever experienced their kindness and attention. I liked listening to them talk about which stores might stock suitable clothes for me, as nearly everything I wore had been made by my mother on her Singer treadle sewing machine or was a hand-me-down from my sister. Not that I had any excuse for complaining. My mother, even for women of that time, was talented at sewing, and she crafted numerous garments for me.

With the main bombing over, the high street shops were back open for business, with the damaged ones temporarily boarded up. After so many months of constant jeopardy, just getting out and walking with my aunt and uncle was a joy. Without the threat of sirens, I found my ears could once again tune in to the hum of the crowd. People had returned to browsing and chatting and were more animated and obviously happier than before. As we started our latest expedition in Clapham, I pointed up to the streetlights.

"What are they for, Uncle Douglas?" I asked.

He couldn't help but chuckle. There'd been no street lighting for two years, so I only knew them as something I could use to tie my skipping rope to.

With the barrage balloons all fat and glossy in the sunshine that day, even the sky appeared benign. It completely escaped my mind that the real purpose of the balloons was to deter low-flying aircraft. Of course, London continued to be on high alert, and walls of sandbags remained in place around important buildings and men in uniform stood on guard on most street corners. Another reminder of how close we'd been to an invasion were the tank traps – great slabs of fudge-like concrete – that had been temporarily shifted to one side at the top of the main streets to allow the buses to pass.

As well as being connected to the church, Auntie Vi was also a leading light in the local operatic society. We spent a number of evenings sat around a baby grand piano listening to her sing songs from *The Mikado*, although when the mood took her, she was quite at home with more light-hearted music hall favourites such as 'Put on Your Ta-ta, Little Girlie.'

As the theatres had started to reopen, I was treated to my first ever trip to see a show, a production of *The Student Prince*. Auntie Vi couldn't have picked a more enthusiastic companion. Having never seen anything like it before, I found it utterly mesmerising. I was starstruck from that very moment and had found the answer to what I wanted to be when I grew up. Once home, we continued to sing all the songs from the show, with Auntie Vi playing the piano and Uncle Douglas serving us drinks. When it was my turn to play, I couldn't understand the muddled black blobs on the sheet music paper, but I still enjoyed placing a sheet on the stand and bashing away with gusto. I fell asleep that night on their feather-stuffed sofa, which I found so warm and luxuriant compared to anything at home that I immediately vowed I would own a feather bed one day.

From Auntie Vi, I also got the opportunity to learn more about my relatives. She told me about my grandfather, whom I'd never met as he'd died in 1930. Back then, photographs were less common, and I'd only seen one picture of Philipe Braunstein as an old man. He had a devilish-looking beard and a few remaining strands of grey her. My aunt told me how he'd been a successful businessman and had expected his sons to join him in the family ink and printing trade. However, when Horace and Phil abandoned the business to join up at the outbreak of the first war without his permission, it created a big rift.

When my father eventually returned home from the war after many months convalescing, he would sometimes wake in his sleep screaming the house down. Even worse was when Auntie Vi told me that rather than showing him care and sympathy, Grandfather Braunstein thought it all terribly shameful. Putting his foot down, he declared that he wouldn't tolerate what he considered to be such foolishness under his roof. A chill went down my spine as I thought of my poor father being stretchered away with his lungs full of mustard gas only to then be treated so badly once home. I'd never got close to extracting those more intimate stories out of my dad, and I subsequently considered my grandfather to have been a terribly heartless man.

With good care, my strength was restored and I returned to my parents armed with a bag of new clothes and a pocket full of sweets. I blundered into the house, almost looking through my newly returned sister, and began singing the praises of my aunt and uncle and going on about what a wonderful time I'd had. I just couldn't help myself. It all came out before I could think. Being starstruck, I kept turning the conversation back to the theatre and what the performers wore on stage. As a result, the atmosphere turned sour on a day that had held so much promise.

Of course, I was glad to see Pam, my old sparring partner, but she looked decidedly more adult than before, and the distance between us was now even greater. My parents, clearly hoping for something different, then declared it had been a bad idea for me to go away and have my head filled with nonsense. I was told to go to my room and try on my uniform, as I was starting a new school the next day. Mum later referred to Auntie Vi as an old maid, which I didn't understand although I knew it was mean. When I tried to defend her, Dad divulged that Vi once called him a rough diamond and looked down on us because he was only a painter. The conversation stopped dead, and my dad looked very awkward. He couldn't even claim to be an artist anymore, and when I returned to school, he'd be leaving the house to take up more factory work.

Chapter 10
Buying a Spitfire

Having moved up to middle, or what we called primary school, I had a new set of teachers to contend with and felt at an immediate disadvantage, having missed the first few days of term due to my convalescence. The pupils were divided into houses with serious sounding names: Stevenson, Purcell, Shackleton and Turner, and each of us was given a small metal badge to wear. This all seemed much more grown up than at my previous school. My badge was green because I was in Turner, and for a while I thought this sub-division might serve to be important. However, I quickly learnt that it didn't seem to matter what house you were in. It was only significant when we played sports, something that was low on my agenda.

The school was led by the formidable-looking Miss Clay, with her iron-grey hair and round-rimmed spectacles that she used to examine you more closely if you were unlucky enough to catch her attention. She was a different kettle of fish to the kindly headmistress of my early childhood.

Miss Clay took no prisoners, and it was made clear to us that she believed in running the school as some sort of extension of the war effort. High on her list was for us to be the first school in our area to sacrifice part of our playing fields for vegetable patches. We might not win the area hockey tournament, but there would be wheelbarrow loads of carrots. She also started every day by making the whole school sing 'There'll always be an England' or 'He Who Would Valiant Be'. Like many, I actually enjoyed these rousing songs, particularly compared to the traditional hymns at my last school. Often, we would get quite carried away, and I'll admit to the odd tear in the corner of my eye as we belted out these songs at the top of our voices, as if sheer will could bring down a German bomber.

Seeing our enthusiasm, Miss Berry, the music teacher, stood up at assembly and asked if anyone would like to audition for a choir she was forming. I didn't need to be asked twice. Whilst I knew I wasn't the best singer, I felt that if I projected a confident, strong voice, the teacher would see me as an asset and place me front and centre. After lessons that day, I gave it my best shot and, after listening to my voice, Miss Berry frowned a little and broke the news to me that I was an alto. This was like being told I had an obscure blood group. She explained that I could join the choir but that I wouldn't get to sing the melody. When my face dropped further, she pointed out that I could add a richer sound by supplying the harmony, and that my tone was more akin to that of Vera Lynn's. To be compared to Vera Lynn, the 'Forces' Sweetheart' and already endeared to all Londoners, well, that was Christmas come early. Who wanted to sing the silly melody anyway?

But singing wasn't going to lead to victory against the Germans, and so we were expected to bring things into school to help with the war effort. This we did unquestionably, as we saw it as our patriotic duty. We followed instructions to collect and bring in silver paper, and in our classroom, we had an ever-increasing ball of it, although I was never quite sure what it was for. Despite money being tight for most families, we were encouraged to save regularly at school by purchasing 'savings stamps' – 6d for a blue one and 2s 6d for a red one – which were stuck into our savings books. On reaching a particular total, these could be exchanged for a savings certificate. I remember we had a cardboard cut-out of a British soldier placed in our school hall for 'Salute the Soldier Week', where each time a certain amount was reached, his right arm was duly moved up a notch until eventually, with the total met, he saluted us. It was a proud moment. A more sophisticated version soon followed known as 'Savings Weeks', when a school or a town was set a particular target. Having harangued my parents, I would come to school with a handful of additional farthings to help our school buy a Spitfire or some other war-related item. My mum made little purses with straps that we called 'pussbags', and these were just the job for carrying a hankie and my savings stamp money to school. As young children, we liked to believe that our small contributions were making a big difference, although my dad was less convinced as to where his hard-earned money might end up. On the first of these collections, I felt hugely disappointed to learn that our Spitfire wasn't actually going to visit the school before being sent to war.

In terms of academic matters, the transition between infant and primary school felt like a chasm to me, particularly in those subjects I had previously enjoyed. I used to love collecting things for the nature table and showing off any interesting finds to my friends. This was replaced by something more serious called biology, and overnight, everything had turned into the study of blood, bones and dead things. With a war going on, there seemed plenty of that everywhere else one looked, so I couldn't see the point in having to delve into the ugliness of such matters any deeper.

My only strong academic subject was English, and my compositions were quite often read out in class. This was my saving grace. If I could keep achieving in this subject, it might just paper over the cracks of my failings elsewhere.

I was losing my grip on maths, which is something that has followed me all my life. To me, an abacus had been a colourful wooden toy to play with, not a counting device. I can say that I was genuinely useless at the subject. Back then, there didn't seem to be any identification of the problem, as classes were so big and there wasn't any additional available help. During the 1940s, it was very much sink or swim. I even developed my own coping mechanisms. One frankly stupid example was that Mr Adams, our jocular maths teacher, had proudly boasted at the start of term that he was exactly six-foot tall, which was quite an achievement among a generation of stunted or war-crippled men. So, I decided to use him as a yardstick, and in my mind, I would imagine him lying on the ground or curled in a perfect circle as I tried to work out the length or circumference of a shape. On the odd occasion where I got a sum correct, I'd be let down by not being able (or willing in my case) to show my workings.

So many lessons in general were frustrating due to the lack of materials to work with. Books were passed around until they literally fell to pieces, and pencils had to be inspected by a teacher to ensure there was nothing usable before a replacement might be granted. Even the school ink was made from a dollop of blue powder mixed with water but without the properties of real ink. And so, after having dried for several weeks, like some secret agent's ink from a spy novel, everything we'd written became practically illegible.

Art classes were particularly annoying for me because such basics as paper were considered too important to waste on the brushstrokes of small children. (In school, we had taken to drawing extra lines in our exercise books as well as smaller margins to make our paper go further.) I so wanted to produce something that I might be able to bring home and impress my father with, because I could feel within me that I had some of his talent. Yet the paper that was provided to us in the art class was oddly thick and speckled and clearly not the right material for painting. We were forced to share brushes, paints and a pot of water between three, and so anything that I might have carefully created quickly formed into a blobby, expanding mess. It was like trying to paint on blotting paper.

With the lack of materials available, our art classes quickly regressed into handicrafts and design. My hymnbook cover, in a delightful shade of taupe, was always falling off because I had sized it incorrectly in the first place, my arithmetic letting me down again. And when those materials ran out, I found myself once again collecting leaves around the playing fields and sticking them onto card, which was the sort of thing we had done in infant school. I was too embarrassed to bring any of those babyish examples home.

I largely managed to stay out of trouble, although on the few occasions I sat outside the headmistress's office, my knees would knock together in involuntary spasms. On entering her lair, just one look at the cane, which was mounted behind her on the wall for full effect, had me reeling. Fortunately for me, it was the boys who regularly took a beating – a girl had to do something really bad to get the cane. I remember receiving a good telling off for some misdemeanour or other and promising with all the sincerity I could muster that I would not need to be sent to her office again. I gained the clear impression that Miss Clay really didn't think much of me, and I received a noticeably cool reception from her when I won a book prize at the end of one term. Through somewhat gritted teeth, she thrust a sepia book of illustrated birds into my hands and said, "See how many of those you can spot in London." I'm not sure what I ever did that was so wrong.

Whilst I avoided the cane, I did once receive a proper beating from Miss Moorhead, who took us for games, another subject I didn't excel at. One day, she stood with her back to us drawing an elaborate diagram on the blackboard to represent the tactics she expected the netball team to deploy. Then she announced with a sweep of her chalk that she was going to appoint a games captain. As she declared, "My captain for today is...", I had no hesitation in mouthing to the girl next to me, "Mary Jackson", who was well known to us all as Miss Moorhead's favourite. To clarify, while I'd meant to mouth it, I was incapable of anything resembling a whisper and instead broadcast it to the world. Not appreciating my sarcastic comment, Miss Moorhead flew into a rage and proceeded to pummel me with her fists in front of the standing class. As she vented her anger, she shouted that I had no team spirit or sense of competitiveness. I'd never been hit like that before and was too shocked to cry. Despite the pain, at least I'd enjoyed some sort of minor victory, as Mary Jackson was made captain.

Of course, Miss Moorhead was correct in her observations. I remained short for my age and found netball an absolute bore, never getting my hands on the ball and showing great relief when the whistle was eventually blown and I could sit down again. Even when I was watching and meant to be cheering on my classmates, it was all a bit of an act. On sports day, I would dutifully sit on the sidelines shouting, "Come on, Turner", but I couldn't have cared less and clearly wasn't fooling anyone. And it wasn't just netball, as I really didn't like anything athletic or even going outside in the cold weather. I was usually second from last in the running races and remain forever grateful to plump Sylvia Robins for saving me from total failure. One particularly memorable entry from Miss Moorhead on my school report read, "She seems to be afraid of falling on her head." You bet I was! I had no intention of completing a handstand against the wall and couldn't imagine why anyone would think it was important to my education or the war effort.

My error was that I hadn't quite appreciated how many class friendships and the year group pecking order were heavily influenced by who was good or bad at school sports. In my year group, we seemed to have a proliferation of leggy, strapping girls who stood out on the sports field. Clearly, some children were doing just fine on their rations. They left me for dust. Lacking in team spirit was considered a sin, and not wanting to watch the better girls play netball or hockey meant I was becoming edged out to the periphery. This situation had taken me a little by surprise because I'd believed I was generally liked, or at least that had been my impression from my first school. I started to realise that standing in front of the class and acting the fool might get me a few laughs and some brief acceptance, but it wasn't the same as having deep friendships. When I thought about it, not only had I missed a lot of school, I'd also probably spent far too much time playing board games with my parents and thinking of them as playmates. In reality, my mother and father were only trying to keep my attention diverted, and I was probably under their feet to the point where they were relieved to see me back at school. I considered the situation over the next few days, and although uncomfortable, I resolved that I wouldn't let it fester and would think of a creative way to fit back in and win over more friends.

My parents must have sensed that I was less than happy at school, although I wasn't going to tell them about my problem with maths. With a war on, my issues were quite unimportant compared to what we were going through as a country. The unwritten code of the time was that we had to grin and bear our lot.

Sundays were usually good days at home. Things went at a slower pace, and everyone was chirpier. To help cheer me up, my father offered to take me out on another of his day trips. This time, he decided to take me fishing, something totally new to me and rather enticing. I leapt into action and followed his instructions, beginning with digging up worms in the garden and putting them into an old jam jar. Having changed into scruffier clothes that my mum said I could get dirty, we took a short bus ride and then walked for about half a mile clutching our sandwiches, gas masks and the worm jar. On the way there, as we approached some train tracks and an unmanned crossing, my father lifted me up on to his shoulders and I waved at the driver of a passing steam train. I couldn't believe my luck when the train driver tooted his horn in response as this great black beast of a thing sped past.

Beyond the trainline, we reached our final destination, a deep, tranquil natural pond. It was a delightful spot, and the only sign of civilisation I could make out was a golf course in the far distance. The pond had the strange name of Tinky Tonks. At least that's how Dad referred to it. He had an unerring instinct for giving things the right kind of made-up name.

We didn't own any fishing rods and so on arrival, Dad showed me how to pick what he called 'whippy sticks' – slender branches to which we tied our worms and homemade matchstick floats before casting them into the water. The fish must have been laughing at us from under the surface, as they refused to play their part. However, it didn't take long before we started catching newts. The pond was teeming with the slippery little creatures. The males had spotted orange bellies, and the females were plain brown. There were also larger ones with crests on their backs. We successfully transferred several to a large pickle jar that my dad had brought with him in a rucksack, trying not to drop any.

Although I was more than happy with my catch, the highlight for me was when we headed back home and got to the railway crossing again. There were wooden planks between the rails at the crossing point and my father teased me that he had a special trick to show me if I sat down safely on the grass verge. I did as instructed and watched him dig into his pocket before placing a penny coin directly onto the base of the metal track. He then winked at me before scampering over to join me on the verge. We didn't have to wait more than a few minutes before the next locomotive came through, pulling blackened cars piled with coal. For a moment, I was worried that our penny coin might somehow trip up that great train, but of course, it trundled past us as if we weren't there. We then quickly ran to retrieve the penny, which Dad presented to me all squashed and still so hot that I had to juggle it for a moment.

Dad was grinning from ear to ear at my wide-eyed expression. "It's now your lucky penny and there's no other one quite like that," he said. I turned over the coin again and again, examining the expanded flattened metal. When he finally remembered his parental responsibilities, he warned me, "Don't ever do this yourself, this is just between you and me."

I carefully deposited the coin in a deep pocket, and we set off for home together, happy with our morning's efforts. My mind was already elsewhere, thinking about school tomorrow and how interesting the coin might be to my classmates.

When we got back to the house, the immediate priority was how to deal with our newts. Mum could only watch out of the window with a look of despair as my dad found a galvanised tub and greased the sides of it to stop our catch from escaping. To be fair, he attempted to make it an attractive home for them, adding some rocks and pond weed. I was no expert on newts, but they seemed quite happy. Of course, by next morning they had vanished, and for several weeks I looked enviously at the houses that I knew had the fanciest ponds, thinking that my newts had abandoned us for better prospects elsewhere!

*

While everyone was relieved the bombing was over for now, it did have one drawback. For many of us children during this time, the walk to school had meant scouring the pavement with keen eyes for shrapnel and arriving for registration stiff-necked. With the Blitz over and all the building sites cordoned off, what were we supposed to do? Back at the school playground, I pulled out my lucky penny like a rabbit from a hat and could feel a surge of people drawn towards me. When I proclaimed that my penny was both unique and lucky and how, if they dared, they could make one themselves, a noticeable ripple passed around and I could clearly see that I'd piqued their interest. All day, between lessons, my classmates wanted to see the coin again, and soon everyone wanted one for themselves. Having a lucky penny to protect you might be considered an attractive insurance policy. But really for a group of children who had spent months ducking bomb blasts and collecting jagged shrapnel, it was probably the whiff of danger that was the most compelling element. For the next few days, I was at the centre of attention and could walk a little taller.

Chapter 11
Hard Winter

An enduring memory from the middle war years is the terrible winters alongside the sense of total darkness. At the end of each school day, I hurried home in the blackout as fast as my feet would propel me to avoid them turning into blocks of ice. Once my dim bedroom light went out, I was shrouded in total darkness again, only to awake to yet another coal-black morning. Our house was semi-detached, which was a step up from our previous terraced house, but for me, on a practical level, it meant that my bedroom had two external walls. Central heating didn't exist and so my only source of warmth was a small fireplace in my permanently cold room. The rule appeared to be that a fire wasn't lit in the room until I was ill, rather than putting on the fire to stop me coming down with something in the first place. Of course, it was all down to the cost and availability of fuel. So many miners had been called up to fight that coal had been added to the ever-growing list of rationed items. Such decisions had a greater effect on places like London, as you couldn't exactly wander out with an axe and chop down the nearest tree, which is what I imagined happened in the countryside.

Then there were baths! My mum used to light the Valor stove in the bathroom, and apart from the interesting pattern it made on the ceiling with an accompanying funny smell, you would never have known that it was on. Pam had first dibs, and I'd wait for her to get out, frustratedly looking at the clock while knowing the water temperature would be lukewarm for me at best. Eventually, when it was my turn, I would sit there partially immersed while making a pathetic attempt to scrub myself down with a red bar of carbolic Lifebuoy soap. I knew I wouldn't be allowed to leave the bath if I didn't pass the test of smelling of disinfectant. The water would get colder and colder until I couldn't stand it any longer, and then I'd shout at the top of my voice until my mum would burst in, yank me out and rub me up and down with a small, bald towel. Once I was reasonably dry, she would sometimes brush my hair with the dreaded scurf (dandruff) comb. I don't think I had any scurf, but she insisted on using it anyway. It was a nasty, spiteful thing with fine teeth on both sides and it all but scalped me, leaving my ears tender and pink for ages afterwards. I would whimper over the misery of it all.

The winter that gripped us in early 1942 is now recognised as one of the coldest on record, which seemed like an additional cruelty inflicted on me. A few people remain hearty whatever the weather, yet I could never abide the cold. The only break in this dull routine was when it snowed, and I can remember that winter getting a generous foot of snow, which was more than enough to build a snowman.

My suffering in the ongoing freeze was made worse by our patched-up clothes and lack of calories. Mum believed the weather was "as cold as Hitler's heart", and I sometimes wondered how we would survive and make it through to the spring. We became adept at adding extra tape around window edges and stuffing the letter box to seal up the house like a pharaoh's tomb. Success was measured by how much condensation we could generate, which ran down the kitchen walls once the cooking started.

On one particular Monday morning, Dad's face was set firm as he began wrapping himself in his thickest outer clothes. Braced not only for the cold, he faced new responsibilities at his latest warehouse job. There'd been no shortage of war-related factory work near us, and my father had continually bounced around between different jobs with little enthusiasm.

"I never know whether he's going to turn left or right out of the door!" Mum declared on more than one occasion while clearing up the breakfast things. But only after Dad had shut the front door behind him.

My father disliked the monotony of production line work (such as making artillery shells), and the conditions in those places never really suited his dicky chest. However, he'd fallen into a role that better suited him and involved repairing motorcycles for the military. Someone must have liked his straight-talking manner because he'd just been promoted and put in charge of a small workforce. He would take on these additional responsibilities with few complaints, preferring to be in charge rather than being told what to do. He once confided in me that he would lose his temper with colleagues if they turned up late with a hard luck story or hid in the toilets after a fag break, idling their time away. He had a particular issue with the men who lost all their wages gambling every lunchtime.

Fortunately for my mother, this was at least one bad habit Dad hadn't picked up in the trenches.

Nonetheless, his new supervisory role didn't preclude him from having to work hard. Each night he'd come home, sometimes after a twelve-hour shift, and we'd watch him go through a careful ritual of degreasing himself. It was the same whichever factory he'd been working at, and after a full working day, there was always oil and grease engrained into his face, hands and overalls.

The wages, I'm sure, were welcome, and I believe people were paid quite well compared to factory earnings before the war. Not that there was much to spend your money on. As the war ground on, the rationing scheme kept extending and more and more goods were either unavailable or hard to find.

That winter, Dad regularly brought home broken bits of planking, which he'd smuggled out of work and hidden under his raincoat whilst sitting ramrod straight on the train journey home. Those pieces fed the fire. Once, when we were completely out of fuel, he took a shelf down from the front room, which ended up seeing us through another evening. "I never liked it in the first place" was all he'd say, and who was I to argue? I'd heard about people, often children, clambering under barbed wire fences to get into cordoned-off bomb sites just to steal whatever wood or coal they could find. Such places were unstable, and children occasionally got buried. I wondered how many of our neighbours were feeding their own household items onto their fires now the weather was this cold.

On the way to school, I could distract myself from the freezing temperatures by breaking off icicles from exposed drainpipes and sucking them like lollies. At playtime, I was extremely grateful when snowballs were banned after a window was cracked. Being hit by one left you cold and wet for hours. Of course, I had to keep my wits about me after school, as it became open season, with boys roaming the streets. The ones to avoid were those armed with their 'special' snowballs, which might contain a buried piece of shrapnel 'for a laugh'. It reminded me that 'boy' was 'yob' spelt backwards.

My little gang quickly learnt by copying the children in the years above to construct a shiny slide across the school playground. The polished ice got faster with use, and two catchers were required at the far end to stop any brave user from hurtling into the brick shelter. Without a hint of irony, the teachers spoilt our fun and closed the slide in case we hurt ourselves. Although the Blitz was well and truly behind us, there was little let up in Germany's offensive desire. We regularly experienced what were known as 'tip and run' attacks, when German planes attempted surprise raids to catch us off guard. These weren't the slow and more cumbersome bombers from earlier, but a new breed of fighter-bomber aircraft equipped to travel under the radar and get in and out swiftly.

During one such attack, no one in my household would ever forget the site of a single German plane flying low overhead while making a daytime strafing run up the Great Cambridge Road. I momentarily picked out the whine of an aircraft engine, and before I'd clocked what was happening, it screamed past, angrily discharging its machine guns. I didn't even have the chance to take cover. For a few seconds, all the china in the house rattled, and then it was over. Spent bullet casings littered the banjo, and I discovered bullet marks in the concrete surround of our railway bridge, just a stone's throw from the embankment. (Those bullet holes could be seen for many years after the war, until one day the bridge was finally replaced.)

While the snow was about, all the children played in the banjo after school before being called in for tea. After a few minutes outside, I usually couldn't feel my extremities, but afraid of being called a cry-baby, I tried my best to stick it out. Eventually, I would make an excuse and slink inside to warm up by the stove in the kitchen, before venturing out again all bright and breezy. My friends thought I had bladder problems.

One bitterly cold night, even the cat presented itself in a particularly listless way and I begged my mother to let her stay indoors overnight where she might at least sleep downstairs and keep herself warm. We left Sandy happily stretched out on the coconut matting by the coke stove in the kitchen and went to bed. However, the next morning, we came down to a lounge that smelt of cat pee.

"That thing has to go!" declared my father.

My poor mother did her best to intervene and keep the peace. Eventually, when everyone calmed down, the cat was cast outside, another of her nine lives used up! As well as clearing up after Sandy, Mum already had the extra inconvenience of having to buy 'off the ration' horse meat from the butcher to feed her. This involved boiling the horse flesh on the stove for hours to soften it, leaving a slightly nauseating aroma in the house – few people could spare proper meat for a pet.

It was some months later when the summer sun started to catch that part of the carpet again that the smell brought back a reminder of where Sandy had disgraced herself. Of course, it was all my fault and Mum revealed that 'trouble' was my middle name, which was odd because I knew it was Eleanor.

*

Danger that winter lurked in many forms. Whilst fresh attacks from the air were spasmodic, a deadly legacy of the previous bombing campaign lay underfoot. Attempts at demolishing or rebuilding houses sometimes triggered an unstable bomb buried underground to explode. Many were mapped out, although there were thought to be hundreds secreted below ground awaiting discovery.

On the day I travelled with my school choir into the heart of London for a competition, we got caught in an incident with an unexploded bomb. As we neared the centre of town and our destination, the traffic snarled up before grinding to a halt. Unaware, we amused ourselves on the coach for some time until an agitated policeman began banging on vehicle windows with his truncheon. Cars began manoeuvring, reversing and turning around. I couldn't hear the exact words spoken to our driver, but Miss Berry soon stood up and told us that because a bomb had been discovered, the only way we would make it to the competition in time was on foot. All vehicles had been ordered to leave the area immediately in case their vibrations set it off.

Having abandoned the coach, we lined up in crocodile formation and proceeded to box around a large cordoned-off area as quickly as could be managed. Miss Berry picked up the pace and our gas masks bounced off our hips. Despite more ballet lessons than you could shake a stick at, I was no prima ballerina and had a reputation for thudding as I walked. For some reason, my foot always landed heel first. With a great effort of concentration, I did my best to float along the pavement whilst trying not to fall behind everyone else. To make matters worse, it started to drizzle, and the drops, on the cusp of freezing, slid down the back of my jacket and blouse. Out front, Miss Berry seemed to know where she was going and had no qualms in leading her duckling-like choir girls around the danger zone.

As we got closer to our venue, a large sign erected at the head of a major thoroughfare read, 'Danger, Unexploded Bomb'. Oddly, it attracted more people than it deterred, and all sorts of people trying to go about their business hovered around questioning the wardens about how long things might take. I picked up from listening to the adults that they'd found a 'Hefty Hermann', the nickname for a beast of a bomb, which was nestled underneath a large building. Like most of my friends, I became totally distracted, peering and craning my neck, expecting to see great tail fins sticking out of the pavement somewhere. Of course, there was nothing to see, and all the perilous work must have been happening some distance away and probably underground. A small number of soldiers arrived, stepping cautiously inside the perimeter. Some wore tin hats, which might have kept the rain out of their eyes, but I thought how they would be about as useful as a lead parachute if the bomb actually went off. It was hard to imagine that it was someone's job to share a hole with a grey metallic bomb while armed only with a set of screwdrivers. I couldn't decide if they were fools or heroes.

We reached the concert hall with moments to spare, only to be chaperoned onto the stage in our rather bedraggled state. All I remember of my performance was the sense of expectation, as I waited to hear a large bang at any moment and for the stage to start shaking. We sang our song about a hare in the harebells like a complete bunch of strangers and came last. On the way back to North London, once the coach had warmed back up, we sat there looking like freshly boiled potatoes as the steam rose from our drying uniforms. Our teacher glared at us, as if we'd let the side down.

At teatime, I told everyone about my dramatic trip into town. Dad had a genuine admiration for the sappers and engineers who faced those tasks day after day. He'd seen enough of it in the first war to know the risks.

"Join the army and see the world," he announced, before adding more darkly, "Join bomb disposal and see the next world." He chuckled at his own joke and stroked his whiskers. I'm sure he didn't mean it in a nasty way, and Mum explained it was just an old soldier's humour.

Days after, once the rain had blown through and the wind had dropped to a whisper, a new threat arose – winter smog. This yellow-green witch's brew, combining fog and smoke, drifted over the rooftops, settled in our gardens and passed along the alleyways. It appeared almost to have a life of its own, literally creeping into our house through any gaps it could find, and I swear you could taste it boring into your lungs.

Out came our bag of old towels again. This time, I assisted my parents dampening them under the cold tap in the kitchen and rolling them into snake shapes before pressing them to the underside of the doors in a vain attempt to create an airtight barrier.

Respiratory illnesses were a way of life to us, particularly in the close-knit environment of a city, and we regularly caught chesty coughs that lasted for weeks. More serious conditions like TB were still common, and the treatment for the worst infections was still rudimentary. On top of our own germs, these noxious smogs descended most winters and were a menace to any vulnerable Londoner.

My father was no fool and knew that with his condition, going outside in the smog was akin to playing Russian roulette. Of course, every factory in London remained flat out for the war effort, and our coal-burning power stations spewed out plumes of thick black smoke to keep them supplied. Not fully understanding the association, I still begged Dad every night to put more coal on the living room fire, so no doubt we contributed to the problem as well.

This time, the smog was a real pea souper, and as Dad picked through his newspaper, his features became as taut as one of his stretched canvasses. Back then, most hospitals had sanitoria or dedicated wings just for lung and chest infections, and they were already overburdened with people suffering from complications. We'd watched through the front curtains as an ambulance had called next door, carting off young Fred with his crutches. I never saw him again. I presumed he'd been discharged from hospital and returned to the East End, even though there were precious few houses still standing. I accepted the world how it was and sometimes didn't ask the obvious questions.

Dad kept inside as much as possible, pacing around the lounge like a caged tiger. It must have been another horrific reminder to him of being gassed on the battlefield, and I can't imagine how defenceless he felt. So, when my mum was busy in the kitchen and needed some margarine and flour from the shops, I immediately volunteered my services. Running small errands was one of the ways I could contribute at home, plus, I was sometimes allowed to keep the change. I took a bank note from Mum and picked up my torch before heading out to the corner shop nearest the train station, which was only about a five-minute walk away. Better me than Dad, I thought to myself.

Once outside, my eyes began to water and then the smog caught the back of my throat. It was like standing too close to a bonfire (although there was no fire and it was cold enough to chill me to the bone) and it hurt to draw a deep breath. After a dash down the street, I could make out the dim outline of the corner shop, however, it had shut early and stood dead to the world. Refusing to return empty-handed or have Dad go out needlessly, I braved it through the smothering air, heading further up into town to the Co-op on Leighton Road, hoping it would be open.

Feeling my way under the blanket of smog, I located the shop and gladly completed my purchase before inching out into the darkness to return home. Retracing my steps should have been achievable, but as I could only see six feet in front of me, it all became a little confusing. No, this couldn't be the right way. Somehow, I'd taken the wrong path and ended up down a side street. If that wasn't enough, since the beginning of the war, all the street signs had been removed or painted over to confuse any would-be invaders. With no adults anywhere to be seen and unsure which direction to go, I kept calm and decided to rely on tossing my lucky coin. A squashed king's head would mean left and a flattened Britannia would take me right.

Britannia won the day, and I must have walked a few hundred feet further before I managed to find my way back to a recognisable main road. Since the war's outbreak, all the bigger roads had been painted with white lines down the middle to assist cars finding their way in the blackout. Prior to the war, it was just plain tarmac. What a marvellous invention, I thought, and so I walked straight down the centre of the road using my torch to follow the white lines. Engrossed in my efforts, I barely noticed the occasional car creeping past either side of me at near walking pace, and I'm not sure they saw my small outline at all.

When I eventually made it home, my parents were obviously worried because I'd been out longer than expected. Having confessed to getting lost, they were initially angry with me and then with each other for having sent me out in the first place. But the incident spurred them into the decision that we should escape London at the weekend and go to visit Grannie and Grandpa in Benfleet, Essex. Whilst leisure journeys were discouraged, we knew the air there would be cleaner and worth the effort. I hadn't been out of London for a long time and couldn't wait for a small adventure.

Chapter 12
Clean Air

At the start of that weekend, I awoke to frost on the inside of my bedroom window, something that wasn't unusual. Sitting up in bed to peek outside, I realised the wind must have picked up overnight, as the veil of smog had lifted. This was good news as it meant all the trains should be running. Gathering my courage, I leapt out of bed and grabbed my thick stockings, vest and liberty bodice and yanked them all straight back under the covers in the hope of warming them through before putting them on.

As my only surviving grandparents, Grannie and Grandpa were special to me. They were on my mother's side, which meant she wasn't going to entertain such a trip without looking her best. I loved watching her at her dressing table getting ready to go out somewhere noteworthy, which for obvious reasons had become something of a rare event. Having dressed, my mother's makeup routine was to first smooth Pond's moisturiser on her face before applying lipstick and rubbing it in firmly with her little finger. Then she followed by adding a little rouge to her cheekbones, which she blended in with precision. (In those days, women often had bright red little fingers.) Next, she powdered her face with a lambswool powder puff using her gold compact that would shut afterwards with a satisfying snap.

Pam and I had straight hair, but my mum was blessed with tight natural curls, and as she ran a brush through them, it always amazed me that everything simply sprang back into place. To create extra curl, she would wind her hair around her fingers. She promised me that I could have a perm when I was at the correct age, and the war was over (which sounded like a very long wait indeed). Her final touches included adding a smidgeon of Vaseline to her eyelashes and running a soapy finger across her eyebrows. As this was a special occasion, she dabbed a little scent behind her ears from a bottle branded Evening in Paris. She treasured her scents, not knowing if they would ever get replaced. I could look, but on the pain of death knew I mustn't touch them.

Fascinating to me as this routine was, none of it compared to the business of the tooth. Mum had a loose side tooth as part of her dentures that had a habit of falling out at inconvenient moments. Most days, she was content not to have it in, but today she refused to go to Essex without it. The tooth could only be stuck back in place by holding a stick of red sealing wax over the gas cooker flame and then putting some of the newly melted wax onto it before slotting it into the gap. Whilst she waited for it to harden, she stood over the gas stove, lit a taper and ran it along her arms to singe away any offending hairs (which only she could see). Although mum's hair was relatively dark, she had a sprinkling of freckles that she considered to be blemishes. As the very final addition, she then used one of my father's spare brushes to apply peroxide to those freckles in the vain hope that it would make them invisible. I viewed these last items of preparation with alarm, knowing I had all this to come. I was much darker than Mum.

My father sat in his favourite armchair in the lounge, observing proceedings from behind a cloud of cigarette smoke as all the females ran about undertaking their various rituals. He knew that for once, he was both outnumbered and outgunned, and he had little choice but to bide his time. His own teeth were little better. He proudly told me once that in the last war, when his platoon had been under fire for days and he couldn't report to the medical officer with his toothache, he knocked the "rotten thing" out with the muzzle of his rifle.

For the first time on a long journey, I started to suffer from travel sickness. This was a new phenomenon, and I wondered whether I felt ill because of swallowing all that frightful London air. My parents concluded that it was age-related, as Pam had been the same. I was told it was likely all in my head, which I thought was an odd comment because clearly it was a stomach issue. I steeled myself and tried to talk to my stomach about all the nice food we could expect at Grannie and Grandpa's. As you couldn't turn up at someone's house and expect them to feed you anymore, this also meant bringing some food with us and being ready to donate some of our ration stamps to the cause. It never crossed my mind that the only way these 'extra' ration stamps could materialise involved my parents denying themselves food in the process.

The train windows were hard to see through as they were both dirty with soot as well as crisscrossed with wire mesh in case of a bomb blast. It was an indication that the bombing war was not considered over, just in remission. With my dad's help, I managed to open the nearest window and focused on the loud clackety clack, allowing the crisp, cold air to take the queasiness away. As the train chugged through the outskirts of London, we passed beyond the great ring of anti-aircraft balloons floating over our heads and into the open, clear air. For the first time in ages, it actually felt like we were temporarily leaving the war behind us.

After an uneventful journey and whilst the train commenced recoaling, Dad took me up to the front of the train to show me the engine. He patted the side of it like it was a racehorse. It was not a passion shared by Mum, and so she hung back on the platform with Pam, guarding our bags. Unfortunately, a speck of dirt got stuck in my eye, which was extremely painful. We swiftly left the station with the sound of Mum blaming Dad ringing in my ears, and I was hauled down the High Road until Dad managed to find a chemist shop. He then paid a man a shilling to roll up my eyelid using a matchstick (like opening a can of herring) and wash it out with sterile water. So, five minutes later, when Grannie opened her front door to us and saw my red eye and wet face, she opened her arms wide and I got extra hugs and squeezes, to Pam's annoyance. It had been so long since we'd seen her and so she cooed at Pam and called us "her little broken biscuits" for everything the war had so far put us through.

Being a tiny round lady and not much taller than me, I could bury myself in Grannie's hug and inhale the sweet smell of her smooth skin. It was all I could do to stop myself from stroking her face. Mum had told me that Grannie always kept a bowl of oatmeal and rosemary beside her washbasin, which she applied liberally after washing her face. Another of Grannie's little 'secrets' involved rinsing her hair regularly in beer, so it lessened the grey. I knew better than to ask, as I remembered she also had a fierce reputation if crossed. By contrast, Grandpa was taller and spindly and was all waxed whiskers, silver hair and excitable movements. They made quite a double act on their front step.

Before the first pot of tea had even been brewed, I came under a barrage of Grannie's funny sayings. Back then, many older women embraced folksy wisdom, herbal remedies and superstitions. I was instructed in a very serious manner that I shouldn't cross my knives at the dinner table or pass other people on the stairs. Furthermore, I must never sing before breakfast, or I would be crying before supper. I started to get mental indigestion about the half a dozen rules that would bring good or bad luck to our house. Pam took me aside and reminded me that although Grannie was a witch, she was one of the good ones. At least each individual rule was simple enough for a child to follow. Things got more supernatural with the next edict – that I should avoid viewing a new moon through glass otherwise I'd be poor for the rest of my life. This one sounded very important. The only way to counteract this dire act would be to go outside and turn your money over in your purse. Given I didn't yet own a purse, I wouldn't be in a position to test the veracity of that doom-laden warning.

Lunch would be prepared and served in the front room, and as it hadn't yet warmed up outside, I was allowed to play in there. At least I wasn't going to be expected to entertain the girl who lived opposite, who'd been invited over on my last visit to keep me company. Cynthia, an unfortunate name for someone with a lisp, had been desperately shy and reticent to play. I found her most infuriating. The plan backfired on the adults as they were forced to spend their whole time encouraging her to eat, speak and join the human race whilst she sat in the corner chewing her red hair and staring at her shoes. Thus, in her own quiet way, she'd made herself the centre of attention, which didn't go down well in my book.

If I was going to play alone, I wanted to explore Grannie's large collection of white Goss-crested ceramic pieces. The best items remained locked in a cabinet against the wall and out of bounds to my sticky fingers. However, I was handed a large box full of china wrapped in yellowing tissue, which I enjoyed delving into to determine what was inside. Various pieces jogged my memory and had recognisable chips or cracks that I suspected the younger me had caused. Still, not to worry, that was my old self.

Each delicate item had started life as a souvenir collected by my grandparents on their pre-war seaside holidays. Some were easy to identify, such as the lighthouse, the teapot and the boat, but others were more obscure. There was even a thatched cottage from the Isle of Wight, which got added attention. As the adults stepped around me, I lined them up on the floor, first in order of preference and then alphabetically, according to which seaside town they'd come from, until I finally lost interest and started examining the pictures on the wall.

Grannie stopped what she was doing for a few minutes to scoop up all the china and explain to me how each picture told a little story. They had names such as 'Over the Garden Wall', 'Fisherman's Wooing' and 'Curiosity'. My favourite was 'The Persian Girl', which depicted a young woman dressed in exotic clothing gazing at some goldfish in a bowl. Grannie divulged the secret that they were really all advertisements for Pears soap and had been given away for free, which sounded fantastical to me. Only by examining them carefully could you make out the word 'Pears' skilfully concealed within each picture.

Various platters of food started to appear on the table, and I certainly wasn't disappointed by the lavish spread, which included a variety of sandwiches, cold cut meats and a selection of iced buns. There was even the novelty of a sort of cream topping on a cake, which Grannie explained was achieved by asking a local shopkeeper to keep a tin of evaporated milk in the fridge, after which it could be whipped up.

During lunch, a rather depressing conversation took place about the progress of the war and how Singapore had just fallen to the Japanese. I couldn't tell you where Singapore was, but I thought it terribly sad how we could lose an entire country like that. And then, inevitably, what always followed any adult war talk was a discussion about everyone's health. Dad managed to sidestep the conversation by saying that his chest felt better just by being out of London. He then excused himself for a smoke outside. At this point, the women started to address more personal matters. I don't know why all eyes fell on me when the topic of constipation came up. Pressed by the adults into declaring that I hadn't managed to 'go' for a couple of days, Grannie shared with me that, "It will feel like passing a table leg studded with diamonds!" I instantly regretted devouring more than my fair share of the stodgy cakes.

With a milky sun starting to break through outside, I was happy to escape their examination and play in the large, rambling L-shaped garden. I roamed along the ferns and down to the bottom of the main garden before rounding a hedge and pushing past some straggly trees, where I discovered a huge black car parked up accompanied by four strange men. They were dressed from top to bottom in black, and they frightened and surprised me at the same time. I rushed back to the house to tell Grannie, and she just laughed and explained that Grandpa was letting out that part of the garden to a funeral director and the car I'd seen was a hearse.

"All the funeral directors are in great demand and working seven days a week," she said as she shoved another log on the fire. "It's the cold snap, it's good for business – but they're not having me just yet!"

Grandpa also pointed out that they were still occasionally being bombed and sometimes receiving more than their fair share. In all likelihood, this was because the less fanatical German raiders had developed a tendency to release their bombs over Essex rather than run the gauntlet of London's outer air defences. Before that moment, I'd never really considered that my grandparents were at all vulnerable where they lived.

To lift the atmosphere, it was suggested that I should show Grannie some of my latest sketches. I could tell she was genuinely impressed with my progress when she held Dad in a vice-like stare and said, "Encourage her to follow her dreams." The message really chimed with me, and then she added, "Any morsel of opportunity should be taken."

I'd never heard anyone talk about art like that before. For as long as I could remember, people had always been rather sniffy about my dad calling himself an artist by trade. It was as if he hadn't got a 'proper' job somehow, and that a man with a family should have a regular wage. I decided that I was proud of him and never considered him frivolous. He was following his passion and willing to ignore the naysayers. At the same time, I better understood that I should follow my own path, wherever that would take me. That afternoon, my head was full of thoughts.

The weather outside continued to improve and Grandpa suggested that we should put on our hats and scarves and walk to a nearby pub for some "fresh air". My parents weren't particularly keen drinkers. Mum shared that Dad drank spirits like medicine, in one gulp with a grimace. So, I'm sure this was all about what Grandpa wanted to do, as he liked a pint. Pubs remained open throughout the war, and while beer was never rationed, it was not always available. Sometimes, you would see disappointed customers scowling at a pub where NO BEER had been scrawled on a chalk board. There used to be an amusing cartoon character called Chad (or Mr Chad) that became popular during the war and was associated with the shortages. Chad had a funny face and a long nose and was drawn or chalked looking over walls. Underneath would be the words, "Wot, no petrol", "Wot, no sweets", or sometimes, "Wot, no beer". Basically, whatever it was that was in short supply at the time. As children, we thought Chad was great. He was a rather rebellious character who captured our sense of humour during the darker days when we had little choice but to put up with our lot.

Grandpa wasn't to be disappointed, as the King's Head was open and doing good business. Pam and I were made to sit in the pub garden whilst the adults enjoyed a blazing fire inside. I didn't complain too much as there'd been a turn in the weather and it felt a touch milder. I was handed a bottle of something described as grapefruit juice. This sounded very tropical to me, although the drink had clearly not been produced with any real fruit. Disappointed, I thought my silvery-grey fizzy concoction tasted of soap. When Dad appeared a little later, he brought out a packet of crisps for us to share, which really was a treat because they were the plain ones containing a pinch of salt in a blue packet. During the war, these were as rare as hens' teeth. I had to confess to him that I didn't like the bubbles in my drink and so, using an old trick, he dropped a coin into the glass. Unfortunately, it didn't do much to improve the taste, although when I tipped the drink away later, the coin was welcome.

When it was time to go home on Sunday, Grannie handed my sister and me a small gift each. As I thanked her, I added, "I wish I could see more of you." Her sharp reply was, "Well, I'll take my clothes off for you next time." How could I not love her? I recall all the adults then having a deep discussion as to whether I'd travel better by a window seat. I wasn't paying much attention at this point, reckoning I'd feel nauseas wherever I sat. On the journey home, Mum found an envelope in her bag, and I was distracted for quite some time by tearing it into small pieces, sprinkling each handful out of the window and watching the breeze take it away. Eventually, I fell asleep lying across Mum and Pam.

I was still half-asleep as we ambled home in the failing light, Dad carrying me on his shoulders for the last leg from the train station. Walking at night was a hazardous occupation at the best of times, even when you knew the territory. Suddenly, Dad lost his footing on what might have been a stubborn patch of ice and we both fell through a bush into a neighbour's front garden like a couple of drunks. Valerie Braunston definitely doesn't like standing on her head. With no light to guide us and no railings to hold, it wasn't an uncommon occurrence. As he wrestled with a climbing rose before brushing himself down, Dad used some swear words I hadn't heard him say before. Mum completely ignored him and rushed to my aid. I was fine, just a bit shocked. Of course, all this was achieved using hushed voices, as it wasn't the done thing to cause a scene in front of the neighbours. That's what common people did, and we had standards to keep up.

However, worse was to come as my parents held their torches at our door and fiddled with their keys in the dark. Opening the front door only revealed that disaster had struck whilst we'd been away. The water tank in the loft had burst, turning our stairs into a waterfall and leaving a cold, soggy pool on the carpet and kitchen tiles. Everywhere was dripping and wet, and seeing our home damaged this way disturbed me in a way I can't easily describe. I'd been braced for such things during the bombings, but this event had totally blindsided me. I was rather undone by it all.

The rest of my family rallied around, pulling up rugs, tidying and getting a fire going to help dry things out. I was encouraged to go to bed and get out from under their feet. Fortunately, my bedroom was unaffected, and I sought the sanctuary of my soft toys and familiar things while inviting sleep to come. Grannie had talked about following my dreams, yet from that night onwards, my dreams often became more fitful and complicated.

Top left: Valerie at 6 months old. Top right: Valerie, moving day to Bush Hill Park.
Bottom: Valerie on the day she moved to Bush Hill Park.

Top left: Horace (right) with his brother Phil, having both just enlisted.
Top right: Horace (top far right) and 'The London Boys', Flanders 1917.
Middle: Horace, between the wars, with his Hitler moustache.
Bottom: Horace (second left) at a munitions factory.

Top left: A school photo of Valerie. Top and bottom right: Valerie and Smokey.
Bottom left: Horace and Valerie.

Top left: Grannie and Grandpa from Essex. Top right: Grandfather Braunstein.
Bottom left: Pam at 18. Bottom right: Pam (left) with Valerie.

Top: Family picture, Isle of Wight holiday, 1946.
Bottom: Post-war family photograph.

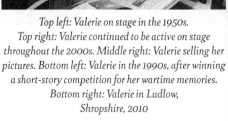

Top left: Valerie on stage in the 1950s.
Top right: Valerie continued to be active on stage
throughout the 2000s. Middle right: Valerie selling her
pictures. Bottom left: Valerie in the 1990s, after winning
a short-story competition for her wartime memories.
Bottom right: Valerie in Ludlow,
Shropshire, 2010

Top, middle left and right: Blitz damage, Bush Hill Park, published courtesy of Enfield Local Studies & Archive.
Bottom left: V-2 damage, Bush Hill Park, published courtesy of Enfield Local Studies & Archive.

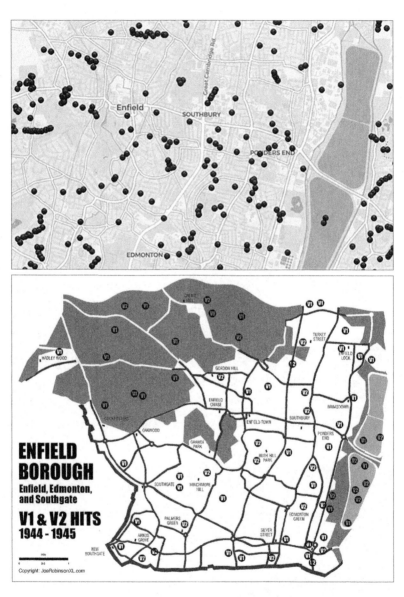

Top: Blitz map of Enfield, published courtesy of Bomb Sight and The National Archives.
Bottom. V1/V2 Map credited to Joe Robinson.

Chapter 13
Bobbie Comes for Christmas

As the summer months ticked by and the days shortened once again, I found the descent towards another wartime winter hard to take at times. Although we weren't under any immediate threat, there seemed to be a general lack of joy in the air. With the Americans finally having entered the fray and their might deployed around the globe, war blighted every far-flung corner of the world. Battles raged and I couldn't tell if we were winning or losing. This had truly escalated into a world war.

With the latest school term over, I was once again left to my own devices, and I found myself oddly fascinated, perhaps unhealthily so, with the post office despatch riders who came around the streets. Everyone knew that more often than not, telegrams contained some terrible news about our serviceman fighting in faraway places. Nobody wanted a telegram anymore. Those yellow envelopes were delivered with greater precision than a bomb, and each one could snuff out a life. In our family, with no close relatives in the war, I should have been able to relax more, yet I found myself drawn to the window every time I heard a motorcycle nearby. And it wasn't just me. Around the banjo, curtains twitched, and nervous faces looked out each time a young rider slowed to check a house number. My parents tutted, scolding me that I shouldn't get involved in other people's business, but I couldn't help imagining myself living next door with the Clements family and being on constant tenterhooks.

My parents responded by vowing to pull out all the stops to try and make this season's Christmas a special one. We all needed the distraction. Shop-bought decorations had become expensive and hard to find, providing an artistic family like ours the welcome challenge of making everything from scratch. Our house was swiftly decorated with paper chains, and even the inside of the blackout blinds benefited from a Christmas-themed makeover. My task was to craft a small tree for the table using a pack of pipe cleaners, which kept me engaged for a good day.

For some reason unknown to me, there were always pieces of rectangular cardboard loose in the bottom of Shredded Wheat packets. This year, Dad had insisted on saving them in case they might be useful for something. He then proved his point by painting Merry Christmas on each one and stringing them up around the house. It was also his job to make the homemade crackers, which would set off our table nicely.

One of Mum's tasks was to make the Christmas pudding, which took up a whole day. I was excited about the sixpence secreted in it and thought that coins should be added to every dessert. Just as all the preparations had won me over and got me into the holiday spirit, I could sense it was Mum's turn to be agitated about something. Her key concern was about what meat would be available for the main course. There were no such things as freezers and we didn't own a refrigerator, so even if something suitable did turn up by chance, we couldn't have stored it. (Any meat we could procure was kept in a 'meat safe' at the bottom of the garden, which was essentially a box cupboard with a mesh front to keep out rats or foxes.) Dad told her not to fret, determined that he would sort something out when the time came. Mum wasn't convinced, as all anyone talked about were the shortages and how Christmas would be the most difficult yet when it came to food. The pressure was on Dad to deliver.

During that period, a man used to visit, whom Dad instructed me to call 'Uncle Vic', even though he was another non-uncle and probably just an old wartime pal. He gave the impression of being a bit of an artful dodger and was memorable by the fact he both had a car and access to fuel. To this day, I don't know whether he managed to get petrol through legitimate means or if it was to do with the 'black market' I'd heard so much about and was keen to visit since it stocked so many unavailable things.

Uncle Vic picked up Dad in his car on a bright but chilly day to collect holly from Epping Forest with which to decorate the house. Pam and I came along for the thrill of it. I enjoyed zipping around in a motor vehicle and taking corners at speed, which was a particular novelty compared to our ponderous local buses. We parked next to a large clearing that was apparently an abandoned encampment. Uncle Vic explained that during the Blitz, the area had been used as a temporary camp for people to escape London at the start of the bombing. I didn't envy anyone hiding in a forest with only branches overhead as the bombers circled.

I'd visited a few places beforehand that had been referred to as a forest, but nothing like this. I found the tall trees, the rustling and the way the light was cut out a little disconcerting. It had a way of forcing me to gawp up all the time for threats that weren't there. Neither did I relish getting separated in the dank undergrowth, so I stuck close to the adults as we began gathering our greenery. Foraging for spindle berries, I'd hardly got one in my hand (let alone near my mouth) before I was told they were poisonous and could kill me. The next instruction was to make sure I didn't get raked over the eyes by the sharp bramble (nature's barbed wire) that seemed particularly concentrated at my head height. Adding to the growing uncertainty, I was reminded to watch my footing and not step on any metal objects that might be stray munitions. We didn't get as far as warnings about roaming wolves, falling trees or death by lightning strike, but my eyes were already on stalks. On top of this, my socks were sopping wet, and I longed for the reassurance of brick and concrete. I tugged Dad's hand and asked to go home.

*

Thankfully, throughout the war, Christmas Days were full of pleasure, and I don't recall the Germans attacking during that period. I considered whether some of them might be Christians, although from what I'd heard about them, this didn't sound likely, so I put the lack of bombs down to the thick blanket of clouds. Currently, I shared a bed with Pam (which was a practical way to keep warm during the depths of winter), and so on Christmas Day itself, we nudged each other awake early. Enthralled, I examined the two overflowing pillowcases that substituted for Christmas stockings that had been tied to the bedframe. I hauled up my booty and soon Pam had done the same. The age difference between us melted away as we giggled and examined our mysterious packages. Most of our gifts by this time were homemade or second hand because there was little new stock available to buy in the shops, yet that didn't make them any less appreciated. I couldn't understand how my sister didn't instantly rip open all her wrapped presents like I did, and she was happy to hold back and just enjoy watching me make a mess on the bed.

This year, I was hoping for a new pair of shoes, which, like all clothing, was rationed and increasingly hard to find. No one had found an answer to growing feet and so my father had become adept at stretching and mending, which meant I could get a little more wear out of each pair. I recall spending most of the war years with my toes rammed against the inside of a pair of shoes, and it was a miracle that I had any toenails left. And so, I was surprised that my parents had gone one better this time and got me a pair of new, or nearly new, roller skates.

I also unwrapped a ballet dress complete with a tutu decorated with artificial flowers, all made by my mother's ingenious hands. The other item I desperately wanted was a new drawing book of some kind, and Pam had come up trumps. My artwork was constantly improving, and I had a vociferous need for more material. It was noticeable how thin the paper was this year, and at my first dashed attempt to colour something, my pencil went straight through the paper. Indeed, I had to be careful simply turning the pages as they ripped so easily. I would need to take a breath and develop softer hands – artist's hands.

Pam gladly received a songbook from Woolworths with all the words and music for the latest tunes on the wireless. Her book was the star item that early morning and something we could share. We had such fun in our room, beating out the rhythm of a song on each other's bottoms and trying to guess the tune while trying not to wake our parents.

Christmas also meant that we would eat lunch in our vastly underused front room. Ours was particularly well-decorated, and my dad was proud of the three-piece suite he'd acquired before the war in beige uncut moquette. It sat in front of a fawn-tiled fireplace surrounded by various brass ornaments. In retrospect, it seems odd having your best possessions in a room that's hardly ever used.

The only problem with our front room was that the fire was notoriously difficult to light. Dad took off his coat, and despite it being Christmas Day, he began to curse as he prepared to do battle with the inferior-quality coal. Pam and I watched him struggle for ten minutes with a box of matches, his face down in the hearth and choking on old soot. It was like trying to bring back the dead. All we could hear was his theories and explanations about angles and airflow, which went right over our heads. His next trick, which he promised he'd seen work before, was to stuff newspaper up the narrowest point of the chimney to block the airflow and draw the draught. He then took a step back and lit the newspaper. Fully engrossed, we saw the paper turn brown, then red, before it suddenly burst into flames, prompting Dad to jump forward with the tongs and rapidly dump his homemade incendiary device on to the coals below. This also failed. Refusing to be beaten on Christmas Day, he stomped out of the house, and I thought he was going to come back with an anti-aircraft shell or something similar to throw on the fire and blow us all up. In fact, he'd only gone to the shed, from which he returned with a can of paraffin that he liberally tossed on the fire that had remained ever-so-slightly alight. As the fire finally exploded into life, it almost took his eyebrows off. Fortunately, Mum was in the kitchen working on the lunch and missed all the antics. Dad wiped the sweat from what was left of his brow, streaking his face with a line of black soot, and gave us one of his 'don't ever try this' looks.

My sister was of an age where she wanted fashionable clothes and beauty products rather than toys, which was a tall order during that period. In retrospect, I feel terribly sorry for her, as the war must have robbed her of so much pleasure. What Pam really desired was a new bathing costume for next summer, as squeezing back into her old costume for another year would have been, quite frankly, indecent. Given that all the swimming baths had been shut for the duration, she must have had her heart set on the various rivers and ponds that were so inviting on very hot days and where lots of the boys hung out. Never one to shy away from a challenge, my mother did her level best to try and produce another miracle with her sewing machine. Terry towelling was a highly absorbent material with lots of uses, including that of sanitary wear. Presumably, this was why it was one of the few materials that could be readily bought in the shops. Having sourced the material, my mother then worked incredibly hard while Pam wasn't around to design a two-piece swimsuit. By proceeding to embroider it with red daisies, she tried her best to disguise its origin.

When the front room had warmed, Pam decided to go upstairs and quickly change into her new costume to show it off to us. Of course, my father had taken no interest at all in the garments my mother had secretly slaved over and hadn't even seen this particular present before it was wrapped. And so, when Pam entered the front room with her hands on her hips like she was on a catwalk, he blurted out, "Why are you dressed in a baby's nappy?" Fortunately, Pam was generous enough to see the funny side and we all fell about laughing.

I'd been asking for roller skates for ages, having tired of seeing my friends race past me as I breathlessly tried to keep up. The best place for roller skating was the station concourse, which was perfect today as there were no trains running. I wasted little time in trying them out before Christmas lunch, which never got going before mid-afternoon in our house. The station and surrounding shops were as quiet as a graveyard, and for a split second, I was transported back in time and had to check myself, worried that I'd missed a siren and that everyone had already scarpered for cover.

Getting my wits back, I commenced skating up and down past the shop fronts. I was cheered by the seasonal displays in each front window, in what was a collective act of normality. At the confectionery store, great Cadbury's and Bassets boxes suggested mysterious pleasures, although I knew they were empty and only for show as I recognised them from previous years. I tried not to let the boxes taunt me.

After an hour or so of roller skating, I'd worked up an enormous appetite. In London, we couldn't get whole turkeys or chickens anymore, but this year we did have a large, succulent rabbit with all the trimmings. I did it full justice and ate everything in front of me, and there was even enough meat left over for a rabbit stew the next day.

It was years later before Dad told me the awful truth. At the time, some of the men where he worked kept a few geese and rabbits out the back for their meat. Lots of them had little sidelines going to help make a few bob, and Dad was as active as the next man. Some nights he came home with a random bag of vegetables or some extra ciggies that he'd received in exchange for something like a pencil sketch of one of the men's children. What I particularly enjoyed hearing in the months leading up to Christmas were his entertaining stories regarding Bobbie the rabbit. This infamous animal had apparently become really tame and affectionate, and all the workers petted and looked after him. He even had his own hutch built from some spare wood to keep him separate from the other animals. The stories about the scrapes and incidents involving the bunny with a larger-than-life personality became more and more elaborate, and Bobbie turned into something of a hero to me. But without me knowing, that Christmas, the men had held a sweepstake, and Dad had won Bobbie, which he subsequently smuggled into the house in secret. And so, Bobbie became the centrepiece of our Christmas dinner. My parents knew full well that I wouldn't have touched a scrap if I'd known.

One sad event from that festive period involved Sandy the cat. Just after Boxing Day, she got into one fight too many, and a wound on her front paw became an abscess, which we only knew about when she started to limp. Dad fretted because it was the Christmas period, and he doubted whether he'd be able to find a vet's that was open. To his credit, he knocked on doors and asked around, eventually hearing of one that hadn't shut up shop. With great care, he placed Sandy in a large cardboard box and took her away. The outcome was something I was totally unprepared for, because when he returned carrying the same box, I assumed he had brought back our cat. Instead, like some outlandish conjuring trick, he opened the box and out stepped a greyish-blue Persian cat with round yellow eyes and a huge plume of a tail. For Mum and Dad, it was instant attachment, whilst I was left gobsmacked.

Apparently, the vet had told Dad that Sandy needed to be put down, but he was so impressed by the lavish care we'd provided for the old reprobate that he was sure we could give a good home to another unclaimed cat that he had out the back. I'll never know how my father could be so disloyal and move on from our loving furry companion in the flick of a switch. Crossing my arms, I stubbornly refused to have anything to do with this interloper. Of course, he was such a beautiful looking creature and so affectionate that I could only hold out for a few days before accepting him dearly. We named him Smokey. I helped to brush and comb him, and I became an expert at teasing out the hairballs that he was prone to develop in his coat. Despite struggling for meat, we all pledged to sacrifice from our rations and give him the best homecooked food we could manage, as well as cutting his meat into little pieces, as befitted such an aristocrat.

Chapter 14
Sweet Farewell

By summer 1944, the war had been raging for several years, and in some never-ending test of endurance, my entire life revolved around rationing, blackouts, empty shops and the constant reminder to lug my gas mask around with me everywhere I went.

It was beyond belief that in recent weeks, the Germans had chosen to recommence mass bombing raids. As a family, we tried to stay resolute. Nighttime attacks returned with an aching familiarity, only now the sizeable raids were more scattered than before. Lacking the same punch, Londoners quickly showed their distain by dubbing the campaign the 'Baby Blitz', although perhaps not the ones who were directly underneath!

Like most children, I'd developed the knack of being able to identify different types of aircraft by their engine noise as well as sensing how near or far they were. I remained alert, ready to hide under the stairs – my first port of call – at a moment's notice. Fortunately, North London was largely spared and I avoided spending any nights in the Anderson shelter. Most evenings, I would bury myself deep in my bed, my poor soft toys losing their shape under my weight, and try and sleep to the backdrop of guns and distant bomb strikes. When sleep wouldn't come, I'd sometimes sit up and play with my flattened penny, turning it over between my fingers and reminding myself I had extra protection.

On occasion, the Germans braved it in the middle of the day as well. When a pesky, single-engine plane flew directly over our part of town it triggered the sirens, prompting Dad to groan, "Someone needs to shoot that poxy thing down. How are the night shift supposed to get any bloody sleep?" I wasn't sure if Dad was being sarcastic or not, as the greatest din came from our own ack-ack guns as they blazed away at the daredevil flyer to the point where the house shook.

The number of British guns had steadily increased since the original Blitz, and it was no easy task for any German to take on the protective 'ring of steel' now encircling London. Old enough to clamber on to the shed without Dad's assistance, I gazed upwards and watched the plane escape eastwards through a hail of black puffs from our guns. It was surely harder to miss him than to hit him. Then, if that wasn't enough, RAF planes arrived to chase off the intruder, with their own guns chattering. I felt a rare stab of sympathy for the outnumbered German pilot trying to cut and run before the Spitfires or Mosquitos could mob it and bring it down. It didn't seem a fair fight.

The Baby Blitz faded away and I was mightily relieved that the Luftwaffe had been seen off, at least for now. My thoughts turned to more promising days ahead and my growing obsession with food. It wouldn't be a lie to say that it was the first thing I thought about on waking and the last thing on my mind at bedtime. Not only was I half-starved in the womb, but it was as if dark forces were still conspiring to restrict my calories. Just the merest whisper that a shop might have packets of currants or some broken biscuits to sell meant people would line up in the street for opening time. My mother's life year-on-year was little more than a daily existence based on queuing, queuing and more queuing. And when it got to her turn, just because she was in possession of the right coupons or points didn't automatically mean the listed items were available. Frustration was rife, and it appeared the government's only answer was another campaign of posters to put some backbone into the home front.

"Back them up!" was the latest slogan, accompanied by an illustration of our brave lads fighting overseas. It seemed to be trying to shame us into not moaning, but I wasn't so easily gagged!

Our official rations, when first launched, were intended to be balanced and adequate, yet they'd subsequently trimmed back our allocation several times. At what point would they be declared 'inadequate'? Not only did we get fewer of the basics like cheese and meat, but more everyday items were added to the ever-growing list of rationed foods, including children's sweets. How dare they! My mother kept asking what magic trick was she meant to perform with her one precious egg per week? For me, the lack of variety was the hardest thing to take. Of course, nobody starved, as long as you didn't mind potatoes cooked in half a dozen different ways.

Once the warmer weather visited us, I would make a detour on my way home after school via the allotments on the George V playing fields. Now these emergency allotments had matured, it was easy for a young, short-for-her-age girl to wander through the greenery, where I might tuck into the occasional pod of peas, which were sweet and tasty in my sugar-starved world. I would pop open the pods and pour them into my mouth, being careful to check for the odd maggot that might have found its way into my snack. If I could have gotten away with it, I'd have helped myself to more, but these allotments had become a lifeline and were understandably well-guarded by the people tending their respective patches.

One day, I came back from the allotment having plucked some strawberries, which were the holy grail of homegrown fruit, all without being seen. In my haste to stuff the delicacies into my mouth and assuage my hunger, I'd squirted copious amounts of red juice over my face and down my clothes. When I waltzed into the kitchen, my mother shrieked, momentarily horrified that I might have been blown up. I felt terribly guilty, even though the strawberries had been particularly delectable. It was all a stark reminder of the hair-trigger life my mum led, trying to keep me safe with a war on.

Somehow, despite fate's best endeavours, I'd managed to grow a little taller, and when I studied myself in Mum's full-length mirror, my features were more defined. Mum caught me looking and unhelpfully told me what I already knew. "You'd be a good two or three inches taller by now, if we'd got all the proper food. Still, there's always time after the war." Then she turned to Pam and said, "Luckily, you had all your big growth spurts before rationing came along."

Pam smirked and patted the top of my head, emphasising my smaller stature. I wondered if it really would be possible to catch back up again "after the war" – so many sentences started with the words "before the war" or "after the war".

I wasn't the only one getting older. My parents also presented themselves to me as more aged, but in a less favourable way.

Life for them remained severely pinched, so perhaps worn out was the best way to describe them. When I watched my mother heaving another basket of wet washing outside to the mangle on a fine day, her back looked stooped, and it made me want to run outside to help. Dad's hair had also thinned out, and it didn't take much to tip him into a bellicose mood. Noticeably, he would sit with a watery cup of tea, complaining that Mum had reused the tea leaves yet again. To Dad, a proper cuppa was one thick enough that it would hold his spoon upright.

"I've lived through ten years of war," he complained one day, during one of his regular bouts of melancholy. "Something should be done about the politicians who've led us down the garden path." He banged his rock-hard biscuit down on the side table to dislodge any weevils. Of course, there were no weevils, and it was an old habit he'd retained from being in the forces. Pam placated him whilst I didn't waste the chance to swoop down, vulture-like, on his crumbs to eat them before anyone might notice.

My father had even abandoned his "every day is jam" saying, which was meant to cheer us up. Sugar had become unobtainable, and I was told to sit down and make do when Mum put a ghastly jam substitute made of mashed parsnips, swede and food colouring on the table. Like some form of make believe, we all took turns spooning it on to our bread and pretending it was fine. It would've been terribly ungrateful to my mother to have made a comment as I knew how hard she'd tried.

So many of our recipes were full of substitutions. My mum used to cook our dinners using favourite recipes that she had snipped out and saved from magazines and newspapers. As the war progressed, she scratched out ingredient after ingredient and replaced them with substitutes. By now, her recipes had become more pencil amendments than original recipe. Even the government started publishing books and pamphlets for families about how to make mock chicken pie and mock plum pudding.

We sometimes had to face my mother's attempt at homemade sausages. They would be so heavily laced with pepper and spices to try and disguise their unspeakable contents that I could only eat them with a glass of water to hand. Even more galling was knowing that the sausage-eating Germans would be sat at their dinner tables with lashings of them.

Noticeably, American soldiers started to appear on the streets, a clear sign of their growing commitment to the European theatre. They stood out with their healthy demeanour and crisp uniforms, and Mum worried me one day when she commented on how solid and firm they looked, as if she was eyeing up a ham shank at the butcher's shop. Alongside these servicemen, their boats brought us tins of sliceable Spam, a versatile food that could be eaten in a variety of ways. It's surprising what you can get used to when you have limited options. However, on hot days, due to the lack of refrigeration, it had a tendency to turn into a greasy soup. This generally meant that in peak summer, when a tin had been opened, you could expect Spam for breakfast, lunch and dinner. (I confess that I can't open a tin of pork cat food without the smell taking me straight back to wartime.)

Of course, the longer the rationing went on, the more susceptible we were to poor health. Waves of bombers were replaced by waves of illnesses that swept through the population. It was during this period that my mother became quite sick herself for the first time in my life. I remember she took to her bed with pleurisy and later was admitted to hospital. I'm not sure I fully appreciated the gravity of the situation. Children weren't generally allowed to visit hospitals in those days, so I have no image in my mind of seeing Mum ill in a hospital gown. I simply remember her absence and the change of routine. I suspect Dad covered things up as best he could with a bit of a story. He tried to make light of things, telling me she'd suffered from the same illness years before when they were first dating and, ever the romantic, he'd taken her upstairs on an open-topped bus, where they'd got soaked on a drizzly day.

With my mother out of commission for the foreseeable future, I was faced with the unsettling prospect of having to report to a neighbour called Mrs Cole directly after school. Due to his supervisory role, Dad couldn't get away early from his war work at the factory – he was expected to be on site before his workers arrived and be the last to leave at the end of the shift.

I didn't know the Cole family particularly well, as they didn't have any children. I'm sure it was kind of them to offer to help, but it meant I had to stay with Mrs Cole at her house until Dad could get home. She was another bowel-obsessed adult who interrogated me every day about my movements – a very awkward conversation to have with a near stranger. Mrs Cole also insisted on me swallowing a full dessert spoon of cod liver oil and malt, which I thought was a revolting concoction.

"Look" she'd say, waving her silver implement, "Mr Cole loves it and even licks the spoon."

I wanted to reply, "Mr Cole can have the whole bottle then", but I was too polite to do so. I kept my fingers crossed each day that Dad wouldn't be held up any longer than necessary.

On the first evening Dad collected me, there was my unabated hunger to deal with. It would have been preferable if Mrs Cole could have fed me more than a spoonful of liquid, although that really would've been too much to expect with food supplies so short. Promptly, when we got home, Dad took one swift look around the kitchen and then told me to get my shoes and coat back on and to bring my gas mask. He declared that we were going to eat out "as a treat". Indeed, I had the same 'treat' every night until my mum got back from hospital. He took me to what was called a 'British Restaurant', which were government backed and had first sprung up during the original Blitz to feed bombed-out families, initially as soup or communal kitchens. Over time, some of them had converted into simple eating establishments.

The one my father took me to was a short journey away and looked and operated very much like a restaurant does today, with waiting staff and menus. I was particularly taken by all the neat tables adorned with their crisp, white tablecloths, the antithesis of the drab streets we'd just walked along. However, it was all illusionary, and I recall being bitterly disappointed that they had no better access to food than we did, so the only meals on offer were identical to what we typically had at home, such as rissoles or minced beef (and don't ask too many questions about the mince). Every main dish on the menu came with the ubiquitous parsnips, potatoes and cabbage. Even though I was hungry, I pushed the food around on my plate, in the vain hope that a waiter might bring out the real menu and surprise me. Dad shot me anxious looks across the table and urged me to eat up, but I just couldn't whip up any enthusiasm for what was on offer. I'd never seen him look so relieved as when he finally bought Mum home from hospital.

Around this time, Pam turned 18, which meant she wasn't at the house much to help either. Everyone reaching that age, whether male or female, was expected to do their bit, and she was as keen as the next person to contribute. Initially, she toyed with joining the Women's Royal Naval Service, or Wrens as they were affectionately known, for little better reason than that she liked the uniform. This didn't land well at home and my parents worked hard to dissuade her. As the war progressed, more and more women in uniform were backfilling for the men, and Dad was concerned she might be sent abroad and put in harm's way. His view was that once you'd signed on the dotted line and put on a uniform, you were under the King's Regulations.

In the end, things took a lucky turn, and she secured a job in an Enfield town department store. Such shops remained open with a skeleton staff as retail was considered an 'essential occupation'. Thus, unlike so many of her friends, she avoided being drawn into the forces or grinding factory work. This was fortunate for Pam because the factory girls worked long hours in often dark and sometimes quite poor conditions, spending their days with their hair tied up in the dullest of clothes. Pam was never a dungarees kind of girl. By contrast, she was expected to look presentable for her shop role and now wore lipstick, nail varnish and had her hair in sweeps at the front and the rest rolled around a ribbon. Mum made her two brown dresses that she wore on alternate days, spiced up with various jabots at the neck and fancy lace cuffs. When she left for work on her first day, she looked more like twenty-eight to me than eighteen.

In the evenings, Pam would regale us with stories about dealing with difficult customers and her floor supervisor, Mr Benson, who hovered in the background because he had a badly scarred face due to cowpox. Some of Pam's salary was commission based, and so she wasn't taking home much money, particularly as she was on 'third sales'. This meant that when they had a customer in their section with money to spend, two of her colleagues were ahead of her in the rankings. But even with only modest earnings, she no longer had to rely on my parents, could contribute to the household and would largely come and go as she pleased.

Here again, the gap between us grew ever wider. Pam wanted to be sophisticated and meet young men, whereas I was still too much of a tomboy and when not at school roamed the embankments at all hours and lived in shorts. Her job had its perks though, and she used to like meeting the handsome sales reps that would come to the store. Sometimes, they would give her free samples to try out. One day, she bought back a home perm kit, which was a very new and exciting thing at the time. Both Mum and I were fascinated by the process and helped apply it on Pam, only to have our efforts ruined when Dad came home and inadvertently threw the neutraliser down the sink without realising what it was for.

Seeing Pam all grown up, my mother decided it was about time I made more of an effort to appear more ladylike. At the same time, she also wanted to help Pam with her sales commission. One Saturday, I was forced to visit the department store to buy shoes and a herringbone tweed waist coat with a velvet collar and a half belt at the back. It seemed an extravagant waste of our clothing allowance and I hated the whole ensemble.

Surely, it wasn't my fault that some earlier bomb damage at the banjo had been repaired that day by a group of workmen, leaving a section of fresh cement. When I went out with my skipping rope and came back for tea, I was completely oblivious to the fresh grey stripes that I'd added to the back of the new jacket and how my shiny shoes already looked second hand. I'd never seen mum so enraged, and she struck me across the face for the one and only time in my life. Of course, I realise now how much hard-earned money must have gone on those clothes, which hadn't even lasted the day.

The only advantage for me of having a grown-up sister was that she started getting boyfriends. For some reason, she would only date young men in uniform. (It must have been very hard for those single men not in uniform at the time, if lots of the girls thought like that, particularly once the Americans started coming over in large numbers.) Pam's boyfriends were usually on leave, and they arrived and returned to their units with revolving-door regularity. They were always especially nice to me, hoping I would put in a good word for them with my sister. They were fresh out of luck! I usually did my best to jeopardise these burgeoning relationships with comments such as, "You should see Pam with just Pond's cream on her face at nighttime." Yet, it rarely deterred them.

Of course, everyone was aware of why the American forces had amassed here with their abundant resources, and they brought with them an immense sense of anticipation. The war had finally reached a turning point. Like everyone else, I experienced huge joy and relief when it was broadcast that our troops had successfully invaded France in the course of D-Day. Mum had the wireless on from breakfast, and standing in the back garden, I could make out the distant drone of ships' sirens signalling the good news. I skipped to school that morning feeling euphoric like everyone else. We'd been taking it for so long and it was good to feel like we were striking back.

In the immediate aftermath of the invasion, it was no longer some thin-lipped effort to dutifully sit through the evening update from the BBC, trying to hear something positive we could believe in. Following D-Day, our family fought for the best seats next to the wireless. Perhaps I was growing up, but what I remember is the names of several towns in France being read out and the word 'liberated' being used. This was a far cry from Britain's role in North Africa earlier in the war, or, more recently, the coverage of slogging through Burma, which might as well have been on the moon as far as I was concerned. One day, I found Dad studying the atlas with his reading glasses on the end of his nose, sucking his dentures and frowning. Pam whispered that he didn't want to lower our spirits but was worried our soldiers would soon be advancing over the same fields that he'd trampled over not so many years ago. The mood in our house though was mostly good, and more than ever we were determined that we could stay the course. With the might of America behind us, things had surely pivoted in our favour – or so I thought.

Chapter 15
Unnerved

For the first time in my life, events took a sudden and unexpected turn, and I felt strangely broken inside. It all changed for me quickly over the course of just a few days.

Due to D-Day, school that week had started in a celebratory mood, and the playground was alive with positivity. Then, at a routine assembly, we received the news that one of the girls in the year below had been killed playing on some train tracks. I was shocked to the core and stood there shrinking into myself as the headmistress lectured us about the dangers of trains and crossings.

"How many times have I told you... not safe... stupidity... bound to happen."

I couldn't pick out every word – I'd forgotten to keep breathing. I felt for my lucky penny, turning it over and over while repeatedly telling myself it wasn't connected, even though, deep down, I felt the tragedy was all my fault.

The minutes ticked by, and when my eyes were able to focus enough to look around the assembly hall, I saw a great wall of indifference on most people's faces. Even the headmistress was rather matter of fact. Is this how brutalised we'd become? We were in a world where children got blown up or buried, children got sick and died and silly children got hit by trains because they were playing where they shouldn't have been. I tried to pull myself together for fear of giving something away.

The day passed in a blur, and I chose not to talk to anyone about it, even though a great burden of guilt had made its home inside my chest. I was crowded by thoughts about what that child's parents might be going through.

Then, only a week after the success of D-Day, any joy with the progress of the war quickly turned sour as the very first V-1 crashed into the Mile End district of London, killing six people in their sleep. I was aware of the second rocket attack because it flew our way before exploding in open ground at Epping with a distant, ominous thud. Having enjoyed an extended period without any bombing raids, a creeping dread overtook me.

More V-1 attacks quickly followed, and the tension they brought was palpable. What were these new, mystery weapons tumbling out of the sky? People were initially dumbstruck, and I had so many questions that my parents couldn't come close to answering. Maybe Hitler only had a handful of the bombs... maybe that had been the last of them. But the V-1s came buzzing across the sky in greater numbers, hitting sites all around us. The bombing raids of the past had come and gone, but these rockets arrived at odd intervals, creating a constant state of tension. 'Alert' and 'all clear' sirens howled around the clock, day and night, having a debilitating effect on everyone's morale, including my own. The twist of the knife for Londoners was that, yet again, we were the intended target for this new and indiscriminate terror weapon. Having survived the war up until now, I'd done my best to convince myself of my invincibility, but now I wasn't sure of that at all.

Official censorship had ratcheted up to new heights, so it took time for people to reconstruct events from the fragments of doctored newspaper and wireless coverage. (Only much later did we learn that everything was on the hush-hush because the government didn't want precise locations reported, which they hoped would blunt the Germans' opportunities to recalibrate their aim). We knew that Britain still maintained a large volunteer force of observer crews all over the country, whose job it was to stand on roofs armed with binoculars, ready to raise the alarm. Dad liked to point out that they'd spent the summer drinking tea and topping up their suntans. Trained to identify large formations of German bombers, we understood they'd been taken by surprise by these single, fast-flying rockets that had distinctive orange exhaust plumes. Our anti-aircraft guns couldn't hit them and the RAF, having previously won the Battle of Britain and seen off the bombers, couldn't fly fast enough to intercept them. Britain had been well and truly caught with her trousers down, and in London we were back to square one and expected to 'take it' all over again.

In anticipation of sleeping in the shelter again, Dad went to inspect what state it was in. I went nervously with him, whilst he tried to explain the reality of the situation and how this would be for the best. In my anxious mind, that meant burying ourselves half underground in a shelter that had been abandoned to the spiders. When Dad heaved back the entrance cover, we could immediately smell that the floor was boggy from seepage. Just putting my head inside triggered all sorts of miserable flashbacks. With a raw voice, I point-blank refused to go inside. Being older now, I couldn't be tempted with some encouraging words and the chance of a biscuit.

Grateful for small mercies, whenever the sirens sounded, we agreed, on a temporary basis, to go under the stairs. My father worked tirelessly to find new material to try to seal and waterproof our Anderson shelter, fitting some sort of steel tube through the roof for better ventilation. This took him several days and I watched him from an upstairs window, practising my excuses. In my heart of hearts, this was all about buying time because all the tea in China wouldn't persuade me to go back into that thing.

The boom of each V-1 hitting London meant that I could hear the detonation, and sometimes, I even felt the earth tremor. A Heavy Rescue Unit rumbled up the Arterial Road when a rocket fell nearby, well-practised in their mission of attempting to locate flesh and bone under the wreckage. At first, I kept fiddling with my lucky penny, but it failed to stop the explosions. Then I bit my lips until they started to split and bleed. My mother looked gaunt with worry, arguing with Dad about what we were going to do. All the while, the rockets kept coming and coming.

Daytime was a little easier on the mind. Rightly or wrongly, I felt like I could outrun or outwit a V-1 rocket. By that, I mean that we'd all quickly learnt the trick that if you could hear a V-1 overhead then you were fine. They had a distinctive, fast-pulsing engine noise, quite different to an aircraft. (Years later, I was upset one Sunday morning by the sound of our neighbour's new two-stroke diesel engine lawnmower, and it took me a while to realise why.) The rub came with the eerie silence when the engine cut out. That signalled the bomb had burnt through its fuel and was destined to fall earthbound, like a stone. I had about 20 heart-stopping seconds to take cover before the thing hit the ground and exploded.

My dad instructed me that if I was caught outside somewhere, I shouldn't try to make it all the way home and instead run hell-for-leather to the nearest front door.

"Just burst in and fling yourself under a table," he told me. "You can introduce yourself afterwards."

Back then, most people didn't lock their front doors anyway, and when the V-1s came, the consensus was that they should be left unsecured, ready to accept any 'guests'.

Daytime wasn't really an issue for me; it was nighttime I hated. I found myself listening for V-1 engines and then their silence, my brain staying alert and not letting me sleep. Gone were the days when I could drift off in Dad's armchair to the backdrop of cheery music playing from the wireless. I considered that growing up had become something of a curse. And it wasn't just me that was causing a problem for my parents. They were in a terrible pickle because their natural instinct was to protect both of their children, and not only was I refusing to go to the Anderson shelter, but Pam was as well. They had even less control over my sister, as she declared that she had no intention of giving up her new job, which gave her an income and her freedom, to go into hiding.

When sleep eventually came at night, it would be with my knees drawn up to my chest. I wasn't fully aware of holding a hanky to my face and biting holes in it. When my mother found it, she concluded that a mouse or a rat must have been the culprit.

Dad was having none of it and made the point that houses with cats don't get mice, and certainly not upstairs in the bedrooms. I was sent out to play and got the distinct impression that I was the topic of conversation. Kicking at stones in the front garden, I knew that I wasn't quite right. Although I recognised some of my odd behaviours, I was too young to be able to understand that I was unravelling.

Another difficult conversation ensued with Mum when I came back indoors. With her back to me, she continued frying up some knobbly leftover bits of potato and veg in lard – her wartime version of bubble and squeak – whilst pressing me on returning to the Anderson shelter. "Dad says he's sorted out the waterlogging and given it a good once over," she said. "Nearly all the bad smells have gone." It hardly sounded like the Ritz. When she put down her spatula and turned around, she saw me grimace and her pleas became more urgent. "Don't trust what they might be telling you on the BBC," she continued. "I've heard rumours that whole streets are disappearing in one go." Her expression sharpened. "We must face facts – our shelter is the safest place to sleep."

The muscles in my face remained tightly drawn. Without weighing what I wanted to say next, I found myself shouting, "I'm not going back into that hole in the ground." But my defiance was more tearful than resolute.

Something was going to have to give, and that was me. That night, I suddenly woke up screaming. My entire family rushed to my side to wake and comfort me. I tried to hold back my tears, telling them that it was just a bad nightmare and that I'd been dreaming about spiders crawling over my face in the Anderson shelter. Everyone, including me, was shaken to the core.

The next morning, like a bolt from the blue, my mother announced that I was going to join the fresh exodus of people leaving London. Evacuation! This time, it wouldn't be Pam going, just me. I only understood in vague terms. Rather than wait around for official channels, Mum had found someone living well away from the V-1 raids that had a spare room and could take me. I was to pack to leave that morning. She then added feebly that it would only be for a few weeks, though I think I'd willed her to say that. Neither of us really believed it.

Within an hour, I'd packed a single suitcase, and Mum took me to the train to head somewhere we barely knew anything about in the countryside. It was fitting that my escort was a nurse because it had been confirmed that I wasn't well. The distinctive phrase used to describe my condition was that I'd become 'unnerved' by the V-1 attacks. I felt a burning sense of shame. If I'd have been dug out of the rubble and then sent away, I could have held my head up high. And who was this nurse? Apparently, she had attended to Mum in hospital when she went down with pleurisy. Today, it seems like quite an arbitrary thing to hand over your child to a person you'd briefly met in hospital, but with so many people desperate to flee London once again, I guess my mother took a calculated gamble to try and protect me.

In that frantic hour of packing, and with no time to explain, all I knew about my situation was that I was to travel to faraway Lincolnshire. Why was I going there? And where was it? I tried to console myself with the fact that I'd be staying on a farm, and Pam had very much enjoyed her time away, suggesting it was like one great Girl Guides' expedition with her pals. Surely, it would be fine. Yet for me, there was no fanfare of people at the station to wave me off, no Salvation Army volunteers thrusting tea and buns into my hand and no familiar teacher to mind over me. Mine was a solitary affair that involved sitting next to a stranger and feeling desperately sorry for myself.

In my haste to get as much into my overloaded suitcase as possible, I'd just about managed to squeeze in Lamby Lumps and Pussy Pieces with seconds to spare. Dad had made me sit on the case whilst he strapped it shut. When I asked the nurse if I could get my case down from the rack in our carriage and retrieve my soft toys for the journey, the answer was a very definite no.

"But they can't breathe," I argued.

"Stop acting like a toddler," came her curt reply.

She held her eyebrows raised for a considerable period, which made me feel like an inconvenience, and I hoped I wasn't going to be living with her. My mind drifted. The usual feeling of travel sickness that would normally crawl up from my insides wasn't so powerful today. I'd lost the ability to think about anything much beyond my own sense of resignation.

I reared awake from a sporadic sleep when we pulled in at Grantham station. Having changed there for the Lincoln train, I watched from the windows at what seemed to be ever-unfolding farmland. As the unfamiliar countryside sped by, I couldn't help but worry about what I might find at the other end of the journey. It was getting late by the time I tumbled out of the bus at a village that was going to be my new home. It was a place called Brampton; near another place I'd never heard of called Torksey. Here, the nurse delivered me at the front door like a package she was keen to get rid of. Back in London, we used to joke about never wanting to visit World's End at the top of Enfield. I wasn't laughing now. I'd well and truly arrived at the edge of the world.

Chapter 16
Evacuation to the Piggery

In the scramble to leave London and take up the offer of sanctuary, my parents had told me I would be staying with a farming family. I think we all assumed that meant I'd be living in a big farmhouse at the top of a field, which had been Pam's experience, and one she talked fondly about. The supposedly kind lady who escorted me from London did have parents living in a fine house surrounded by fields, but I never set foot in that house and was immediately handed over to a ruddy-faced man with sideburns, whom I was told was called Mr Grant. Once this transaction had taken place, I never saw or spoke to the nurse again.

With a gas lamp in one hand, Mr Grant walked me down in his mud-caked boots to the bottom fields, where he lived in a shack – which, if you were feeling generous, might be termed a cottage. To my despair, where a normal family might have a front garden, here there was a foul-smelling piggery *right* beside the property. I would be living with the pig-man and his wife. Even worse, Mrs Grant had apparently been born stone deaf and could only communicate with her husband through gestures and odd noises. And whilst he shared that he would be out working from dawn to dusk (doing pig things I presumed), I would spend my days with Mrs Grant at the cottage. At this point, I thought my life was over. With his gas lamp throwing odd shadows on the walls, I was shown to a small room and encouraged to go to bed. I lay there in the dark with my eyes shut and my clothes on hoping I might wake tomorrow and discover this was all a huge mistake.

On the first morning, I awoke to pig squeals and other unfamiliar animal noises. I checked the outside through a chink in the curtain and then examined my surroundings. It was as plain as day that these people were desperately poor, or dirt poor to be precise. I'd grown up with the satisfying aroma of oil paint drying on canvas and brushes soaking in pots of turps. At the cottage, what hit me straight away was the overpowering reek of the pigsty. I'd never seen a pig up close before, not even a dead one hanging at a butcher's shop. My only exposure to them was via my lovely wooden farmyard toys and illustrated children's books.

Thoughts of my parents and home played on my mind, yet I found myself overpowered by both curiosity and hunger. I hadn't eaten for some time, and so I slipped gingerly downstairs to join the Grants. I was immediately drawn to the table by the emerging and welcome smell of fresh bread. Without waiting for an invitation, I commenced wolfing down my breakfast in a way that would have earned me a clip around the ear at home. It didn't seem to bother my hosts. As I stuffed bread into my mouth whilst waiting for some fried potatoes to cool, Mr Grant told me a sobering story about the geese patrolling the yard. He directed me to peer out of the window and pointed out the spot where they'd recently killed a stray dog. I learnt that they chased after anyone or anything they didn't like the look of, and that Mr Grant was suffering from a bad back because they'd got to him as well. If he was trying to warn me then he'd done a jolly good job of it. The geese looked almost as tall as I was and immediately terrified me. I decided that if the Germans ever invaded, we should recruit geese rather than rely on the much-derided Home Guard. Subsequently, I always made sure they were nowhere to be seen before I made a dash in or out of the cottage.

You would think that the nature of living in a farming community would mean food was plentiful. Surely the one thing I would benefit from on a pig farm must be the wonderful bacon. My mother had instilled in me the notion that whilst we were struggling in London, countryside folk got their ration *plus* all the food on the farm. She'd often argue vehemently with herself whilst trying to prepare our meal, complaining, "They should try having one onion a week and attempt to eke out a pitiful amount of mincemeat with a cup of breadcrumbs." Mum truly got it into her head that beyond London was some lush Garden of Eden. Well, that certainly wasn't the case here in Brampton. I promised myself that if fate somehow allowed me to get back to London, then I'd happily set the record straight.

Sitting for dinner with the Grants was eye opening, to say the least. As they set their plates down, I couldn't help but be drawn to their dirty fingernails, which no amount of scrubbing would make clean. The oddest dining habit of theirs was that they always served and ate their pudding first, and I was expected to follow their example. Each meal would start with something like a bread pudding, which my mum would consider to be a good way of using up any bread on the turn. I'd certainly never viewed it as the star centrepiece. The main course then followed. When I asked Mr Grant why they ate their evening meal back to front he simply replied in his thick farmer's accent, "So you don't need s'much meat."

Most days, the Grants lived off Yorkshire puddings and fat bacon; great lumps of fat with only a thin vein of pork, if you were lucky. A London butcher wouldn't have gotten away with handing this type of bacon out in exchange for a ration card – there'd have been a street lynching. The other local delicacy was a beige-coloured mutton and potato stew, where the rising steam was a reminder of the freshly deposited pig dung revealed to me each morning when I opened my curtains. As a working man, Mr Grant and only Mr Grant had supper before turning in for the night. This always took the form of slices from a stinky block of cheese not fit for a mousetrap. Mostly, I couldn't stomach the food and would often make do with bread and potatoes.

Like their pigs, the Grants lived in basic surroundings. The downstairs was made up of a single room that contained the kitchen range, a small wooden table and chairs and two well-worn but comfortable armchairs that faced each other. There was no wireless (and of course, no television) and so I could only imagine what conversation the Grants might manage between them of an evening.

Upstairs, there were two small bedrooms with unusually small windows, one of which was allocated to me. The Grants looked out over the big house on what was called 'top field'. My reward was a first-class view of the pigsty. Lucky me! When I asked Mr Grant whether they had accommodated an evacuee before, he changed the subject. I suspect that the cottage wouldn't have passed muster with any billeting officer worth their salt. There was no gas or electricity, so we only had oil lamps for lighting. The kitchen range was a multi-use item, heating the downstairs and all the hot water, as well as being the key item for food preparation. If you needed bread, you baked it yourself. Potatoes were dug from the ground and there was no butcher's shop supplying cuts of meat. Everything we ate came from the surrounding farms or the tiny village shop that only opened half days.

Last but not least, there was just one outside lavvy, a wooden, two-seater design. I would be relieving myself outside, adding to the stink, with the sound of pigs rooting and snuffling freely around the toilet. With little choice but to use the facilities, I was astonished to find they used strips of newspaper on a hook instead of toilet roll. You can bet that was going to be the main subject of my first letter home.

Across the yard from us and diagonally opposite lived the Pilcher family. Mrs Pilcher had no teeth and wore a filthy pinny. I thought she was quite old until I discovered she had several sons, the youngest of which was two. All I got from them were sideways glances, making it clear that I didn't belong here. Like most of the locals I'd seen, they were largely dressed in the same land clothes that appeared to have been fashioned out of sandbags. One day, the youngest boy soiled his trousers, and so his bigger brothers turned a hosepipe on him and doused him with the cold water. Mrs Pilcher didn't turn a hair, and it made me think of my mother, who would have cleaned up the little boy and then put him to bed, as snug as a bug in a rug. I couldn't work out these country people and I instantly had a gnawing feeling for home.

At the end of my first week in Brampton, I raised the question of writing home, stressing to Mr Grant that my parents would worry if they didn't hear from me. With my usual lack of tact, I'm sure I must have sounded like a spoilt and petulant child. Already, I was homesick and miserable, and I suspected I would frequently be hungry.

Rather reluctantly, Mr Grant produced a sheet of paper and a grubby envelope, at which point he stood over me with his oil lamp as I started to write. He directed me to be quick, saying all I should bother with this time was a quick line to say that I'd arrived unscathed. I could always write more next week. He then made me write my address on the envelope before snatching the note back up again and sealing it inside.

*

Having been granted the freedom to investigate my surroundings, I couldn't help but be affected by the beauty of the countryside. It quickly became my consolation. Beyond a smattering of farm buildings, houses and cottages stood a sheer vastness on a scale I'd never seen before. It was so completely different to the tiny parks or slivers of greenery near Bush Hill Park. At first, the simplest of things tickled me, such as discovering the springy village turf, which was bursting with wildflowers and so different to the much-abused grass of North London. It was a release to be able to come and go as I pleased, and I had my first experience of clambering on top of stacked hay bales, from where I could see for miles around. I remember watching in astonishment the last vestiges of a golden sun dipping below the distant horizon. Previously, I'd only ever arched my neck to view the sun blocked off behind tall buildings.

Wherever I went, there wasn't a sandbag to be seen, and nobody bothered carrying a gas mask. It was as if the war hadn't yet trespassed here. Feeling rather rebellious, I left my own under my bed, and for several days, I kept expecting someone in a uniform to jump out from behind a tree, blow a whistle and point out my indiscretion. Also, I hadn't seen a single government poster in Brampton village. It was as if people here could live their day-to-day lives unimpeded. Depending on the weather, I sometimes picked up the drone of Allied bombers in the sky, gathering and forming circles high up before heading east, although I barely registered their malevolent purpose. Aside from that, I wouldn't have known that there was a war on.

Quite close to the farm, the nearby area was dissected by small strips of water called dykes, which were a riot of colour and a source of endless interest. They were filled with an abundance of forget-me-nots, like little blue stars. I also saw my first ever dragonfly, which I was proud to identify from a nature book that I'd brought with me from home.

There was a plethora of mushrooms in all shapes and sizes that I found new and beguiling. When I discovered a copse of trees, I parroted my father and decided to call it Myrtle Grove –the name seemed to fit. It also contained these huge and wonderful birds. Thinking they must have escaped from a zoo and were hiding, I didn't tell anyone in case they came to take them back again. They became a regular part of my daily exploration, and I often smuggled out breadcrumbs for them. I later found out they were pheasants.

Whatever weight I had carried with me from London began to lift. As the weeks slowly drifted by, I started to look forward to getting up in the morning to go exploring after a solid night's rest, and it felt as if I'd emerged through a long dark tunnel into the sunshine.

I did occasionally welcome a companion called Rosemary Dickenson, who was known as Rose Mary by the locals. She was the landowner's daughter and about the same age as me. We got on quite well. I think she missed her sister, who had died of diphtheria ('the dreaded dip') a couple of years earlier. She even walked me to the church to show me the grave and the freshly carved headstone, and she appreciated me helping her to lay some pretty wildflowers alongside it. In those early days, Rosemary drilled me with lots of questions about my life in London and what it was like to be faced with bombing raids. She revealed that she'd hardly ever travelled, and that for her, London and the war was a far-off place. In response, she became all wide-eyed when telling me how a German plane had once dropped a stick of bombs on Lincoln and woken them in the night. She also told me how twelve months earlier, they'd seen a Lancaster bomber with an engine on fire fly low overhead, looking for a temporary landing strip. That was the totality of her knowledge. If I'd have known that the war had hardly touched the people here, I would have brought some of my shrapnel collection with me to show them.

We often met in the late summer sunshine to clamber across fields of feathery-headed wheat and onto the haystacks to watch the sheep dipping and chew corn, which could be ground into a semi-sweet glutinous paste in the mouth. Sometimes, we would tuck ourselves away in the warm straw and giggle, sharing our limited knowledge on the facts of life. On other occasions, we took long walks down to where the River Trent met the local canal. Sitting on the bank at Torksey Lock, we could marvel at the engineering as the bargemen navigated the waters with their goods going to and from Lincoln.

Despite how well we played together outside, it was noticeable that as we got closer to Rosemary's home, the conversation tapered off, and I was never invited inside. In turn, Mrs Grant never stepped over the invisible line and signalled for my friend to come in for as much as a cup of tea. It was as if, by association, I was now one of the Grants and that was my place.

Mr and Mrs Grant weren't directly cruel to me, and they might have even considered they were trying their best. Of course, I knew it was all transactional and understood that they benefited from the money my parents paid them to look after me. However, in terms of trying to settle in, Mrs Grant's deafness was a huge barrier. In that initial period when I first arrived, it was a lonely existence for a chatterbox such as myself. Home rarely strayed from my thoughts. But at least they didn't expect me to do labouring chores, and I suspect my life would have been a lot harder if I'd been set adrift here as a boy. I'd already spotted a number of younger people, possibly close to my age, working with horses and helping in the fields. I reckon the Grants took one look at me and imagined me being trampled by the pigs or dragged across the field by a horse.

Mr Grant tried to cheer me up by encouraging me to visit the pigs with him. Before then, the only relationship I'd had with real pigs was to take any peelings and leftover food down to the large pig bins at the end of the road. Every street had one, although there was precious little that people would throw away. Now I realised where the scraps I and so many other people had taken to the street bins ended up. These farm pigs were huge, noisy creatures, and their filth got everywhere. I never got used to the smell and struggled to find them endearing. The exception was the newborn piglets, which only the most cold-hearted person could fail to soften to. Initially, when Mr Grant first pointed them out, all I could see was steam rising at intervals from beneath the straw, and it took me a while to work out that the little piglets were tucked underneath the sow and suckling their mother. They were rather adorable, but understanding what their fate would be, I vowed not to get too attached. Plus, I wasn't planning on being here long enough to start naming them and making them pets. I was hopeful that the V-1 attacks on London would cease at any moment, enabling me to return home.

I had mixed feelings when the next day, a note was delivered to the Grants saying that I was expected to attend the village school, which was restarting the following week. On one hand, the idea of school presented something familiar and comforting from my former life, yet I couldn't even picture a village this size having one. All I knew was that Rosemary had to get up early every day because she travelled to a private school somewhere in Lincoln. Perhaps there was a miscommunication, and I would be going to school with her. What could they possibly teach here in Brompton?

For the next few nights, I kept tossing and turning in bed, my mind spinning with questions about meeting new children and teachers, and what the lessons might be like. Did they study maths and English or would I be learning farming? No one had mentioned a uniform, and I didn't have my old one with me. What should I wear? I was so used to my mother helping me and telling me what to do, and now I had to navigate these things by myself. On the last night prior to school, I pulled the pillow further over to cover my head, as if that might block out all my questions, and tried my best to sleep.

Chapter 17
Playing Dead

The next day, I was directed to a rectangular brick building in the centre of the village, a little larger than an average London house. I wore my own clothes, although that didn't seem to matter as it quickly became obvious that nobody else wore a uniform either, explaining why I hadn't previously spotted any children walking to school. There were two adults at the entrance, shepherding in about twenty other children of all shapes and sizes, and my presence seemed to cause them some confusion. I'd felt invisible since my arrival, and I did my best to raise a faint smile in their direction. If I'd been part of an official evacuation programme, then I'm sure I would have been seamlessly enrolled at school. Here in Brampton, I was clearly an afterthought.

The village school was totally unlike anything I'd witnessed back at Bush Hill Park, and I didn't know what to make of it. The layout couldn't have been simpler, as it was just one large room divided down the middle by a screen on a set of legs. The juniors were given lessons on the left side of the screen whilst the seniors were on the other side. Of the two teachers, Miss

Cartwright took the juniors and Miss Talbot the seniors. Because neither of them knew much about my attendance, there was a kerfuffle about which side of the screen I should be on. Age didn't seem to be the single determinant.

Initially, I was told to sit on the junior side. It was strange attempting to study whilst trying to block out the noise of the other lesson going on. When I volunteered to the teacher that I owned some books and had actually read them, she instructed me to move to the right-hand side for English lessons with the seniors. That summed up my early days in their school – neither fish nor fowl.

At break time, a sensible little voice in the back of my mind prompted me to gravitate to the older children as a strategy to escape a nasty group of boys. The unruly natives, led mostly by the Pilcher boys, were already addressing me as 'Cockney Girl'. Well, I certainly wasn't one of those. I had a Middlesex address! Some of the others in the younger group then decided that I was 'The Gypsy Girl'. I guess it was because I only had to look at the summer sun to develop a berry-brown complexion. To me, the locals had a thin, pasty-faced appearance from working the fields under wide-brimmed hats, but I certainly didn't want to be considered a gypsy. The only time I'd heard that phrase was in connection with the rag-and-bone man who used to come to the banjo once a week to collect junk. When there were raids on, people worried about such people helping themselves to their possessions in the event of their house being bombed.

Miss Cartwright overheard what was happening and took me aside at the end of my first week to explain why I'd become the talk of the village. "People here are generally uneducated because they're only expected to work on the land," she said, "and it's not their fault they don't take too kindly to foreigners or people with odd surnames."

I wanted to shout, "Hang on a minute, I'm from London!", but I managed to hold back.

"Besides," she continued, shifting to a more disapproving tone, "everyone here still remembers the Blitz, when we were overrun with East End evacuees, who stole anything that wasn't nailed down."

Miss Cartwright barely caught her breath, before adding, "Then the Jews came here to escape the city with all their money, bagging the best places to stay. Brampton may only be a speck on the map, but we don't deserve to be taken advantage of."

Angling her head and half-smiling, she gave me a 'I hope that explains things' kind of look. I didn't know what to say or how to react. I was still too young to have the tools or knowledge to really process it.

The one positive thing to come out of our conversation was that Miss Cartwright put me in charge of the nature table. I enjoyed the familiarity of the task and provided almost all the exhibits myself because the other children didn't seem at all interested. They took their surroundings for granted, whereas for me they were still a great novelty.

Fortunately, I quickly became the star pupil on my junior side of the screen, and for the first (and last) time, I excelled at a maths test. Soon, I was able to escape the nasty boys and permanently move to the senior lessons under Miss Talbot, which was life-changing for me. She was a mature, greying lady who was whippet-thin and perhaps in her sixties, which seemed ancient to me, yet she took a great interest in my schooling.

Under her stiff exterior, she possessed a kind heart and sensed my loneliness. Most importantly, she was the first teacher to ever recognise some talent in me. I began doing a lot of 'life' drawing, and she was impressed by my skills. Considering its remoteness, the village school appeared to have a reasonable supply of paper and paints, until I realised that Miss Talbot was reserving *all* the material for me. She diligently took away any of my half-finished work to protect it, allowing me to come back to it the next day. When I was introduced by her to the poetry of Patience Strong, it inspired my own fey attempts at writing mournful poetry. My teacher indulged me, and the occasional wry smile suggested we'd built a connection.

As the weeks passed at the village school, I found a strange way of fitting in with the senior children and started to look forward to playtime. Because of my 'differences', the older girls made a sort of mascot of me (strange little townie that I was), and when they played mummies and daddies, they always made me the baby. I frequently spent the whole of playtime lying on the ground, swaddled in coats for a bed and being fed apples and sometimes precious sweeties. This way, I got to receive the love and attention I desperately wanted. My surrogate parents went a long way during school days to alleviate my homesickness, although there came a point where Miss Talbot thought it inappropriate and put a stop to our charade.

At next break, the replacement game involved lying down on the playground and this time pretending we were war casualties. Everyone sang a rhyme, the words of which I could never quite decipher as the local accents became impenetrable to me at speed. I just followed suit and flung myself on to the concrete at the end of each verse as we collectively took up twisted body shapes. Among the upside down or angled faces, I noticed the other children repeatedly looking over to check my various death poses. Clearly, by being a Londoner who'd been under the cosh, they considered I had some special insight. After the briefest of pauses, a number would be called out and someone would jump up first before we'd repeat the whole exercise again. I don't know why the teachers thought this game was any more wholesome.

On another occasion that broke up the school routine, we were visited by a medical team, who set up a desk at the front of the classroom. This was all a bit different to the normal humdrum and everyone was excited. One of the gentlemen was in an American military uniform and two others wore white coats and might have been local doctors. To quieten us down, Miss Talbot quickly explained that this newly constructed team were visiting all the schools in the area to assess the health of the children and to distribute, where necessary, something beneficial called 'malnutrition biscuits'. My ears pricked up at the word biscuit, although the other word didn't register with me. We were told to form two lines and then began to shuffle forward for the obligatory prodding and probing with metal instruments. There was no privacy, and everything was done in plain sight. Once we'd been weighed and measured like cattle set for market, most of the children in front of me were granted a biscuit, and there were even disappointed faces from the few who missed out. When it was my turn in the senior line, they took one look at my small frame and didn't even bother with an examination. A whole box of biscuits was brought out from under the table. Remembering my manners, I tried not to snatch the box, although my mouth was already salivating, and

I felt like I'd won first prize in a competition. It wasn't just that I was the smallest person on the senior side, but my weight had reduced further since being evacuated, and I was all ribs and not much else.

Oh, the disappointment when I got back to my desk and took my first bite. Yes, the item in my hand was biscuit-shaped, but it became another cruel joke at my expense because it possessed none of the sweetness I so craved. It was dense and heavy in my grasp, and after several attempts at chewing, all I had was a woody pulp of nothingness clinging to the insides of my mouth. With no water to wash it down with, the contents refused to do the decent thing and be swallowed. A swift exchange of glances showed that everyone else was struggling the same way. As we exerted our jaws in a collective wrestling match, the few who'd come away biscuitless sniggered. With their job done, the doctors packed their things up, looking pleased with themselves, presumably thinking they'd saved the children of Brampton from starvation.

In the early evening, I tiptoed through the muck of the piggery and enjoyed tossing my remaining biscuits to a very grateful pregnant sow gated off to one side. If this wonder food contained lots of vitamins and minerals then I could take pleasure in contributing to her having healthy piglets. With strong, vice-like teeth, she made short shrift of the treats. At one point, I actually thought I heard her grunt thank you to me. I caught myself for a moment and made a mental note that if I started bonding with the animals then I was on a slippery slope and wouldn't escape this place before ending up a farmer's wife.

Not only was I short of nutritious food, but I also felt particularly starved of books. I'd had little room to bring any with me and had already read through my meagre supply. On the senior side of the school, all they possessed was a large, shared atlas. When I attempted to locate Brampton or Torksey on the foldout double-page map of England, neither place existed. That sort of summed it up for me. Seeing me lonely and struggling, Miss Talbot helped by lending me books from her own collection and allowing me to take them back to the cottage. I was very grateful. The first book provided was *Heidi*, followed by *Black Beauty*, both of which I loved. But the real revelation was a charming tale called *The Swish of the Curtain* by Pamela Brown. It was about a group of children who start an amateur dramatics society and perform in their very own converted theatre with a blue door. This book opened my eyes to a whole new world. I'd spent so much time entertaining myself as a child that I'd already developed a ripe imagination and was able to immerse myself in their lives. Once I'd ploughed through the first book, I was made up to learn there were more in the series, and so I dived straight back into *The Blue Door Theatre,* followed by *Golden Pavements,* and, finally, *Maddie Alone.*

I realised through these books that it was not showing off to want to perform in front of an audience. Indeed, it was positively encouraged. My mind spun in circles at the thought that there were establishments in London that taught acting as a subject. Due to the war, I hadn't even been in a nativity play, yet I knew performing was something I wanted to experience. Whilst my school at Bush Hill Park had provided opportunities through ballet classes and their choir, I was neither a dancer nor much of a singer, but deep inside, I felt I could act, if only I could be given the chance. The idea started to preoccupy me.

The only source of communication home was by letter, and I urgently wanted to share some of these thoughts and dreams with my mother. Driving me was the realisation that stuck out here in the countryside, I might be out of range of the rockets, but none of my ambitions could ever be fulfilled. From what little I'd seen, I couldn't imagine Lincolnshire having a theatre.

The thing holding me back was the memory of when Pam had been evacuated, as we'd all gained so much pleasure from her correspondence, which illuminated the darkest days of the Blitz. It felt unkind to upset my mother with my self-centred concerns about how bad things were here and how I needed to be back in London where there was still a world of books, theatres and picture houses to explore.

Mr Grant had made it very clear to me that because of the cost of stamps, I should be restricted to writing home just once a week. It wasn't a negotiation. Given I had no money of my own, I had to comply. Even if my parents were sending me money, I certainly wasn't receiving it. Dutifully, I handed my weekly note home to Mr and Mrs Grant, usually on a Sunday night. They inspected my sheet of paper and communicated between themselves in their own way, with Mr Grant using some of the same grunts and whistles that he used with his pigs – it could have come straight out of Dr Dolittle.

Of course, letters also started to arrive regularly from my mother, and I felt an aching lump in my throat just seeing her handwriting on the envelope. On the first few occasions, I would run upstairs to rip open the letter, hoping more than anything for a return ticket home to tumble out. With each disappointment, I would really try to hold myself together but end up sobbing my heart out.

By the fourth or fifth note from home, I was better able to control this upsurge of emotion. Once I'd had a quick cry, I'd re-read them, sucking every last word out of each page. Yet something nagged away at me, and it took a while to put my finger on it. My mother kept asking the same questions, such as the name of my school. It was a real head scratcher. The penny finally dropped when the following letter included a specific request for the name of my schoolteacher, because I knew I'd addressed that point at least twice before. I painfully inched towards the truth that the Grants must be reading my letters and censoring them, or, more likely, not sending some of them at all. I had no sense that this pricked their conscience. They must have been so desperate for the extra income that they intended to keep me here for as long as they could. How long could they maintain the deception? There was a war on, and with an erratic mail service, it was expected that things went astray. This could go on for months. It was the weirdest feeling to discover that I was little more to the Grants than another animal to profit from. The difficulty in such a small community was knowing who I could raise this with, as what I suspected the Grants of doing would be considered quite a serious accusation for a child to make. It was also something that I couldn't prove, so I realised I was either going to have to find more evidence or outsmart them in some way.

Chapter 18
We Are All Prisoners of War

In mid-October, it had been another ordinary start to another ordinary day when, rather out of the blue, I was told school had been cancelled for a week. The weather had turned autumnal, and it was 'tater' picking time, as the main crop potatoes needed lifting before the first frost. There was no time to dawdle when the nation was half-starved. Despite it appearing to be an urgent situation, I'd either been forgotten about or purposefully left behind. I'm not sure why I was considered so much of a liability.

With everyone called away to the fields, my week was going to be even duller than usual. Whilst I wasn't stupid and realised that potato picking might be an arduous task, it also sounded like it could be a bit of an adventure and might serve to break up the monotony of village life. Being ostracised rankled greatly given the remote prospect of anything interesting happening elsewhere.

On the first morning of the closure, I borrowed one of Mrs Grant's potatoes and played around outside, picking it up off the ground and putting it in a basket. After repeating this several times, I concluded that it wasn't back-breaking work after all, making my exclusion more of a burning annoyance. I even went to the schoolhouse just to check it really was shut. I rattled the padlock in frustration and felt a touch of jealousy well up inside, as I thought of my classmates leaning into their task and contributing to the war effort, whilst I was left all alone. Still smarting and with no lessons to attend, I drifted around the farm in my no-man's-land existence, without any guidance as to what I was meant to do.

Brooding, I decided to explore farther afield in my wanderings. The landscape was one of endless flat fields, cut up by paths beaten down by hooves and wheels, and so it was easy to spot what looked like a military lorry pulling up in a lay-by adjacent to a field. As I continued to approach, the rear flap dropped down and out came about twenty men, all dressed in grey uniform and wearing distinctive red armbands. Although there was almost no cover, I found myself crouching down, unsure of what I might be witnessing. Some men started stretching whilst the others huddled in a cluster, chattering away like magpies. They seemed to be waiting, and after ten minutes or so, a tractor arrived and moved over the field, turning the soil and exposing the potato crop. Tools were passed between the men from the back of the lorry, and each took out a potato bucket. Another man, who must have been the lorry driver and who wore a different shade of uniform, stepped to the side and casually started to smoke. I could see he had a rifle slung over his shoulder and that snagged my attention. He was the first soldier I'd seen since I'd been here. I stayed at a distance and was puzzled as to what they were up to and why they were working on the fields, seemingly under armed guard.

When I asked Mr Grant that evening about what I'd seen, he casually told me they were Italian prisoners of war and they'd been sent to help with the farmwork. This was quite confusing to me. The Germans were clearly the enemy because I'd been on the receiving end of their bombing campaigns, but the Italians were more of a puzzle. At the start of the war, I was certain they'd been on the same side as the Germans, but now I thought they were on ours. Or maybe they weren't on anyone's side anymore. I tried to recall what I'd seen in the newsreels and wished I'd paid more attention. And if they were on our side, why were there prisoners here in Lincolnshire being watched by a soldier with a rifle? Peculiarly, Mr Grant told me this was a regular occurrence.

The next day brought a chilly, misty start that gradually warmed during the morning. I went back to the same spot and there the prisoners were again, this time sitting down and eating sandwiches. I couldn't see anyone guarding them, and with my curiosity getting the upper hand, I moved closer, at which point one of the Italian men spotted me and indicated that I should join them. I approached with some caution while several of the other men started beckoning me over too. They must have noticed my eyes on their lunch because one of them offered me a sandwich and another an apple, and then they started jabbering away at me excitedly in words I couldn't understand. They acted as delighted with me as I was with them.

I returned the next day at the same time, and once again, the Italians were kind enough to share their food with me. They tried to communicate with me with gestures and the odd word of English, and they also showed me worn photos of what must have been their wives and children. Some of them kept pointing to or touching my plaits, and I suppose that with my dark hair and eyes, I reminded them of their own children back home.

One man, who was the largest among them and had a beard and a great big grin, was especially kind to me. To everyone's amusement, he took off his shirt and showed me a tattoo of a galleon on his chest, which he then made to 'sail' by flexing his muscles. I showed them my lucky penny, which was passed around before being handed back with murmurs of approval.

Someone from the back of the group was encouraged forward to attempt a few words of English. At first, I thought he was asking me if I smoked, which I found very amusing. Then, with more broken English and pleading eyes, he indicated that he wanted me to try and get cigarettes for the group. I did my best to explain that I had no money. Back in London, there'd always be the odd coin coming my way from my dad or a family friend, but out here I only had my flattened penny for company. The Italian looked rather deflated, and as he shrugged his shoulders, I said without thinking – and using very simple words – that I would meet them here tomorrow and bring them cigarettes. They must have understood, because they all spontaneously burst into song.

That night, I sat up in bed and thought about these strange fellows and the kindness they'd shown to me. In so many ways, we were all prisoners of war out here in the Lincolnshire fields. I wanted to repay their kindness but regretted giving them false hope and scolded myself over my stupidity.

Sleep was spasmodic, and in the middle of the night, a plan dropped into my head involving the packet of Woodbines that Mr Grant always kept behind the clock on the mantelpiece.

Early in the morning, before anyone else had stirred (which was *very* early on a farm), I crept downstairs in my nightie. With my pulse racing, I stood on tiptoes to reach for the cigarette stash. I took several from the packet before quietly scurrying back to my room.

Later, when Mr Grant had already left the cottage, I sat munching my breakfast of toast and dripping, washed down with tea. Mrs Grant was opposite, and while we glanced at each other from time to time, there was no attempt by either of us to communicate. I tried to control my breathing and act normally, but inside, I could barely wait to secrete the cigarettes into my dress pocket and escape the cottage. I was so excited by now that I neither knew nor cared what Mr Grant might do if he realised some of his cigarettes were missing; hopefully, he might not even notice.

I evaded the geese and walked to the edge of the village before racing to the field where I had last seen the prisoners as if shot from a cannon. But there was no sign of them. There was no reason for panic – it wasn't yet mid-morning and perhaps they were elsewhere. I checked the next field and the one after that, ending up spending the whole day propelling myself along the furrowed tracks. The thrill of the search began to fade as I tired. The brambles and stumps of old hedges increasingly snagged at my lower legs, as if the countryside itself was picking a fight with me. When eventually I could go no further, I sat down to take my shoes off and saw blood in the toes of my socks. Despair settled on my features. My new friends had vanished.

That evening, despite my exhaustion, I pressed Mr Grant as to where the Italians might have gone. He responded that he didn't have a clue, and they were likely miles away by now, as the army used trucks to deposit them all over the countryside, wherever they were needed. He reached for his cigarettes, and if the oil lamp had been any brighter, he might have been able to see my red face. With a practised action, he shook one out of the packet straight between his lips, oblivious to the fact that some had gone missing.

Later, when I trudged upstairs to my room with every limb aching, I realised that I'd forgotten about the cigarettes I'd been transporting all day. When I examined my pockets, I realised they were so crumpled that I couldn't possibly return them without running even more risks. Without a pang of conscience, I disposed of them the next morning the only way I knew how – down the despised lavvy.

It was at that pivotal point that I planned my escape back to London. When Sunday came, I wrote a simple reply home, saying how I'd finally settled in and how much I was enjoying life on the farm. As usual, I handed over the open envelope with my note sat inside to Mr and Mrs Grant, kindly asking if it would be alright for them to post it for me. I then picked up my book from the table and pretended to read. Mrs Grant looked quite pleased as she scanned my letter, and I clearly saw her nod to her husband. He then licked and sealed the envelope and pressed a coin into my hand, instructing me to post it tomorrow at the village shop. I carried on as normal, screwing tight my jaw to hide a smile.

The next morning, I whistled as I got up from breakfast, collected my bag and walked out of the cottage oh-so-casually. Mrs Grant never even looked up from the table. Although the shop was about a fifteen-minute walk through the village, as soon as I could hide behind some hedgerows, I teased open the top of the envelope and inserted a thin strip of paper that read, "Please come and get me. I hate it here. They only have newspaper in the lavvy."

Having obviously convinced the Grants that I was happy with life in the country, I then repeated the same trick a week later, adding the melodramatic message, "I don't care if we get bombed, at least we will be together."

Clearly, my plan worked because a few days later, I was told that my mother was coming to visit and would lodge with Miss Talbot, given the cottage was so small. I'd been to her home on one occasion to return some books and it was lovely. Once part of a monastery, it was full of old beams and the scent of beeswax.

I was beside myself with excitement and did little to disguise my pleasure from the Grants. I'd planned and executed my clever ruse and felt most pleased with myself. By contrast, the Grants looked granite faced. I think we all knew what was coming.

My mother wasted no time and came straight to the cottage, rewarding my giddy anticipation. She could see that I'd lost weight in the last few months, and my already worn clothes were even more ragged. Indeed, my underwear had been washed to the point of nearly coming apart. (As a budding actress, I'd gone for the street urchin look and had put on my worst dress and allowed my hair to fall in front of my face like a mess of unkempt seaweed). The game was finally up when my mother investigated the outside toilet and immediately spotted a suspiciously nice new roll of Izal toilet paper.

I don't think there any need for me to explain my situation further when Mum and I went to see Miss Talbot together. My teacher commented that "I wasn't living in the best of circumstances," a typical term of wartime understatement.

My mother's assessment was more direct. "I suspect she's riddled with worms."

"I think my worms have worms," I added.

That seemed to break the ice, and although I could see that my mother was both annoyed and embarrassed, we parted with Miss Talbot on good terms. Knowing I was going home brought many pent-up emotions to the surface, and I bid a tearful farewell to my teacher who had been so kind to me with her books and support. I promised I would write to her from London.

On my return journey, the miles slipped by easily until we neared London. I'd only been away for a matter of months, but as our train decelerated as it approached a mainline station, it was telling how shabby everything appeared, even compared to when I'd last left. Or maybe it was because I was seeing it through fresh eyes. Passing over a viaduct presented a fresh vista of the damaged streets below. Every building stood blackened in soot or caked in brick dust from the continual years of bombing.

My mother pointed out more areas that had been flattened by the V-1s, and now we had these new V-2 rockets to worry about. She told me that they fell out of the sky with no warning, and it was a total lottery because you couldn't take cover. Clusters of houses might go up in smoke, particularly if a gas main caught it. There was no sense of a pattern or particular purpose, just random bad luck. As there was nothing to be done, it was best to carry on as normal, or what passed for normal in wartime.

Despite what she was saying, I really didn't mind. I was so happy to be back home that I didn't feel at all concerned about V-1s, V-2s or even V-3s, should they be next on the list. My mind was clear of these thoughts. As there were no alerts for these new German weapons, even the issue of the shelter had gone away.

The last leg of the journey was incredibly slow. The bus constantly had to edge around piles of rubble, but at least buses could function. London's tram system had come to a total standstill, having been rendered obsolete by holes or damage. As we neared home, my mother caught me craning my neck to see another jagged mess of shattered houses along one street.

"I just don't know how much more of this we can take," she murmured, more to herself than to me. There was guilt etched on her face in bringing me back to all this.

In some form of role reversal, I tried to consol her. "It's fine, Mum," I said, stroking her hand, "it really is fine." And I very much meant it.

Chapter 19
A New Low Point

I ran into our house, bursting with joy and smothering everyone in kisses. When I finally slowed down and the exertion from travelling all day caught up, it was a pleasure to draw in the heartening sights and sounds of home. Even Smokey the cat recognised me and circled my legs while purring loudly. She followed me into the garden, where I pricked up my ears as the first train rumbled by beyond the embankment. I found the sound strangely reassuring. When I waved to the Clements family next door, Joyce and Vera came outside for a chat and we briefly swapped stories. It was nice to be back, and everyone I ran into was pleased to see me.

Meanwhile, my mother was in the kitchen preparing some food. In a lowered voice, she told me that Joyce Clements next door was 'in the family' way, as we phrased pregnancy in those days. I didn't know how that could be because I'd just had a good gossip with her over the fence and knew she wasn't yet married.

Over dinner that night, I shared all my stories with the family. So much of it was new to them because only a handful of letters had made it from Lincolnshire, and they explained that they'd misunderstood my near silence, assuming – wrongly – I'd been busy galivanting around the countryside. My parents were rather intrigued about how people lived in these far-flung villages and wanted to hear about their peculiar ways. I described to them how mud from the farm was walked into the cottage and permanently caked the stone floor. My mother wouldn't have been seen dead without a clean front step and stated as much. The biggest reaction I got though was when I shared my tale about the Grants' back-to-front meals, which brought whoops of laughter and astonishment. I also told them about befriending the Italian prisoners. I hoped that Dad might be able to explain the situation better, but he knew little of what went on outside the city.

Later, I think we all appreciated crowding around the wireless as a family, which was something we hadn't done in a while. I heard the show *Merry-Go-Round* for the first time and quickly learnt to whistle the opening music, whilst my parents and Pam became hooked on *It's That Man Again,* or *ITMA* as it quickly became known. They listened to the show alongside most of Britain, hooting away before prancing around the room afterwards and repeating catchphrases, such as "I go – I come back" in a funny foreign accent, or Mrs Mop's, "Can I do you now, sir?" If any of it was a bit near the knuckle it went over my head and I blindly laughed, pulled along by everyone else.

With no television, the BBC was still our lifeline to the outside world, and when the news came over the airwaves, it came across as genuinely better. Hitler's lot were being pushed back each day, and it was also reported that the V-2 strikes had lessened considerably. Dad continued to follow our soldiers' forward progress on the map and told me that soon the Germans would be too far back to hit us with their rockets. Then followed a hesitant conversation about the general state of the war and how it might even be ending soon, if only Germany would capitulate. Nobody dared say it too loudly in case by doing so they triggered some late-in-the day catastrophe.

In good spirits, Pam went over to the tall, upright cabinet where my dad kept his pride and joy – his radiogram. It wasn't a complicated piece of equipment and was essentially a gramophone and radio sandwiched together. However, on the top of it was a small, green glass dome that glowed when switched on. I was captivated by this 'magic eye'. I'd heard more and more about television and would sometimes stare at the glass dome, convinced that when we had our own television one day, I would be able to see the radio presenters reading their scripts through it.

Pam took pleasure playing some of our favourite records as well as introducing me to one or two new ones acquired whilst I'd been away. Most were unashamedly sentimental and patriotic, reflecting the mood of the time. There were several Vera Lynn songs that we all liked. My mum particularly loved a mournful Irish tenor called John McCormack singing folk songs such as 'Molly Brannigan', whereas Dad preferred his version of 'It's A Long Way to Tipperary'. However, my new favourite was a scratchy version of Sophie Tucker singing the wonderfully titled 'Makin' Wicky-Wacky Down in Waikiki' because it projected a real sense of fun. I'd never heard the name Sophie before and because she had such a deep voice, I assumed for years that she was a man.

I rested much of the next day, reacquainting myself with possessions I hadn't seen in months and trying on my wardrobe of clothes. Several items of clothing were way too small for me now and my mother's smile somewhat crinkled when presented with this new obstacle to run alongside her other chores. Yet again, she dug out the basket of Pam's old clothes, which she'd kept to one side for me. I picked out a few items and for the next few days, my poor mother began the task of unpicking, cutting and sewing, holding pins in her mouth as she went.

When she stopped for a cup of tea, she muttered to me, "Not much longer now," exhaling deeply and readying her Singer once again. I got the sense that she was talking about more than just the dress. And so, I sat with her, hoping that just being present was a comfort and realising for the first time that my parent's wanted – needed – the war to end more than I did.

*

Later that evening, my heart skipped a beat when Pam came home from work and informed me that she'd heard there were Italian prisoners of war working just up the road in Enfield. Whilst I was looking forward to getting back to school to find old friends and tell them about my time away, I still had one free day left and so vowed to try and repay my debt.

Next day, armed with my first pocket money in months, I walked the short distance to the local shop in town. The lady behind the counter was known as a bit of an old battleaxe, although I could tell she recognised me straight away. Something seemed a bit off with her, so I was as polite as possible. "My dad's asked me to run an errand and get his cigarettes—"

"Been away then, eh?" she interrupted. Without waiting for an answer, she practically slapped a packet of Dad's favourite brand on top of the wooden counter. "I expect you've had a nice time in the countryside whilst the rest of us have been stuck here holding the fort."

It was the first, but sadly not the last time I received that sort of dig in the ribs from someone forced to remain in London for the war's duration.

She slid the money off the counter and into the till before looking over me at the next customer. I took it on the chin. My mind was engaged on one thing and all I could think was so far, so good.

With a renewed spring in my step, I boarded a bus going up the Great Cambridge Road towards Enfield. Bus conductors could be relied upon to be helpful, and this one shared that he knew the whereabouts of the prisoners of war and kindly directed me as I got off. It didn't take long to find a large number of greenhouses. The dark, swarthy men in scruffy fatigues who inhabited them wore the same downtrodden expressions I'd first seen on the Italians on the potato fields only weeks before. Barely moving at walking pace, they wandered around with wheelbarrows and implements, performing what looked like various season-end maintenance tasks. The conspicuous absence of guards wasn't an issue as these prisoners didn't appear to have the get up and go to run away.

I shifted between the greenhouses, searching for familiar faces. When I didn't see anyone I recognised, I considered asking after them and then kicked myself when I realised I hadn't learnt or understood any of their names back in Lincolnshire. These men ambled along, all at the same unhurried pace, and hardly showed any interest in me. Like the weather, they'd gone cold. They weren't *my* Italians.

Crestfallen, I left the greenhouses and found a bench opposite, my focus no longer on the dozens of shapes drifting around in their lookalike khaki. Contemplating a wasted journey and a return home, I soon attracted the attention of an elderly passer-by, and after a brief exchange, he told me that there were also lots of German prisoners of war just west of us in Trent Park, behind tall wire fences. In fact, so many of them were flooding in that the authorities didn't know where to put them all.

"If you enjoy staring at prisoners of war, then the Germans are your best bet," he informed me. "They're more belligerent and will meet your gaze."

Having lost his son in the First World War, the old man disclosed that if the weather was mild, he took his lunch in a paper bag to Trent Park just to go and watch them. He didn't explain why or what he was looking for, and I could only feel sorry for him. I made my excuses and headed back to my bus stop.

The events that day created a new chink of anxiety. If Britain was deluged with fresh prisoners, then perhaps I really could start to believe that we were winning, and the war might soon be over. After nearly six years of fighting, the world beyond had taken on something of an imaginary feeling. I realised that war was all I knew.

*

Returning to school after the Easter break, there was a new celebratory mood in the air and every conversation centred on the progress of the war. Each lesson veered off into a discussion on the latest news and most of my teachers, even the stricter ones, were happy to allow the digression. Every day in those final few weeks, great cities fell to the Allies – Hanover, Essen, Vienna, and then Nuremberg. My whole class crowded around a wall-mounted map as our teachers pointed out the latest places captured. The newspapers used the term 'the race to Berlin', as progress had become so swift both east and west of the German capital. I couldn't recall the British army being able to 'race' anywhere previously.

With Berlin finally encircled, my teacher beamed as he declared "checkmate". There was no likelihood of any reversal in fortune. It was all such a stark contrast to the previous years of war. Yes, our stomachs remained half-empty and there was no respite from the shortages, but the days were warming once more, making these final days easier to tolerate.

Who could forget the day we were told Hitler had died? My dad's *Daily Mail* carried a large headline that simply stated, 'Hitler Dead'. He left the newspaper folded on the kitchen table, headline face up, and it remained there for a week. Everyone believed he'd got his just deserts because of the number of lives ruined.

Those heady days as we closed in on victory were blurred by much darker news of the prisoners kept at a concentration camp known as Belsen. The BBC had already broadcast on the wireless from that terrible camp about the plight of Jews transported there alongside various other enemies of Hitler. It was the first time the British people had learnt about what the Nazis had secretly been doing all over Europe. Then a Pathé news film started being shown in the picture houses. It was this graphic newsreel that caused so much controversy because for the first time, the public could actually *see* what had taken place there. At the time, there were reports of people walking out of cinemas or fainting. Some people even argued that it shouldn't be shown at all because of its distressing content.

It's not clear to me why my father chose to take me to the pictures when that now famous newsreel was shown at the end of our film. As he didn't warn me in advance, perhaps he was equally surprised or didn't know quite how harrowing it was going to be. It's safe to say that I can't remember what the actual movie was that day, and I doubt many other people would remember either. It's a trip I've never forgotten.

Up until that point, the worst acts of war known to people in our country related to the Great War. Each town and village had their own grey stone memorials, and between the wars, those solemn commemorations were meant to underline that such things as Tommies drowning in the mud at Passchendaele, or the horrendous casualties of the first day of the Somme, or the use of poison gas, marked low points, never to be repeated. Such depravities were recorded in poems, books and a few grainy images, although generally they were rarely spoken about. Of course, those memories also resided with the men who had been there.

Here, in the comfort of the Savoy Cinema on Southbury Road, I sat in the audience spellbound. I saw through pained eyes those indelible moving pictures of bulldozers pushing emaciated bodies into piles. Other human skeletons staggered like puppets before they too fell. The accompanying commentary talked about the attempted annihilation of a race of people and what

Nazism was really about. It was as if a new nadir for humanity had been reached.

My father sat in stunned silence long after the newsreel ended. Other people around us left in tears. We stayed in our seats for ages, and I didn't know what, if anything, I should say to him. Somewhere in my father's mind, alongside his own war and family secrets, he must have found another place to store and seal up those new images, and I thought nobody should be forced to keep doing that. We sat in the near-empty picture house as staff swept up rubbish around us. I couldn't disturb him in any way, just in case he broke.

I realised that day we were shared witnesses to something I would have to bear with Dad my entire life, and in a step change, I'd also grown up and wasn't his little girl anymore. The war might be ending, but things were no longer as easily defined as winning or losing.

Chapter 20

Coming Face-to-Face with Hitler

So, this was the day we had all been praying for, the 8th May 1945 – Victory in Europe, or VE Day as it quickly became known. Everyone was laughing and crying because our loved ones would be coming home (although sadly not in every case). It was crystal clear that from now on, everything would be different.

As if we hadn't lost enough schooling during the war, we were all given more time off for the celebrations. Of course, I thought this was thrilling, because we could expect street parties in every corner of Britain. I cajoled my mother into making me a new frock because practically everything I owned was plain. I had my heart set on a white dress. Everything in my childhood had been about 'practical' colours and clothing that wouldn't show up stains. My mind was settled on white, as it was the colour of peace.

Keen to please, my mother caved in to my request and, having procured some white sheets, got swiftly to work. She suggested a red checked collar to liven it up a little, which sounded like a sensible idea. When she sat down again at her sewing machine to review her efforts to date, she added check sleeve edges as well as a pocket on the bust. It all looked quite nice until she twisted my arm into agreeing to a check skirt "so as not to show the dirt". In the end, the only hint of white left on my special new dress was the bodice.

The banjo was the ideal place for a party, and it soon became unrecognisable, with every Union Jack we could get our hands on flapping out of top windows. Out of nowhere, red, white and blue bunting appeared, strung between the lampposts. Someone had managed to borrow a collection of various trestle tables from the church hall, and everyone contributed a mishmash of chairs to go with them. The men and the bigger boys prepared a bonfire in the middle of the banjo and the women retrieved every last item they had been saving from their pantries to bake themselves into a frazzle. I'd never seen so many sausage rolls, jellies, blancmanges and cakes in my life.

On VE Day itself, we listened to the daytime broadcasts from the BBC before sitting down to our street party feast. In the evening, everyone threw open their curtains and turned on every light just for the hell of it. The bonfire was then lit, and someone must have opened a window and cranked their gramophone to full blast as music rang out. We were soon tripping over crates of beer as the singing and dancing began. I watched my dad, unshackled for once, dancing a 'knees up' with Mrs Clements and making a complete idiot of himself, although who wouldn't want to let their hair down after six years of such a dour existence? Then it struck me that when the last war ended, there'd been no victory parade for him as he'd been laid up in hospital.

Jessie, Ruby and Pam had attracted the attention of a group of Irish labourers who'd been working nearby clearing bomb-damaged buildings, and they were happily jigging away, dancing their feet off. Little babies were being passed from lap to lap by all the happy spectators.

I quickly befriended one of the happy-go-lucky Irishmen, who introduced himself as Connor. "Isn't it wonderful," I shouted over the music, "we are no longer at war."

"It's not Ireland's war, Missy," he retorted, "it's England's."

How very strange, I thought. It's been a world war and we've all been in it together.

Through a toothy grin, he asked me, "Do you want to see something special?"

How could I resist? He beckoned me up the steps on to the Great Cambridge Road, where I saw the strangest of sites – Hitler suspended from a lamppost. The effigy had a noose tied around its neck and was surrounded by a mob. Some threw beer at it while others slapped its feet, cheering as it pitched left then right. I wasn't expecting to come face-to-face with our arch nemesis, certainly not in Bush Hill Park. More jeers went up as someone attempted to swing from his leg, unintentionally pulling it off. I couldn't say if this was harmless fun or whether it had a more vengeful undertone.

Connor tugged at me, encouraging me to keep moving. We waded through a tidal wave of civilians and servicemen in all variety of uniforms swarming along both the pavement and the road and bouncing off each other like sparks. As far as the eye could see, every face was full of joy. Drunk revellers held up the traffic as we crossed the road, and tonight nobody cared. It was as if everyone had gone rather crazy and awakened something deep within. For me, after six years of following rules and having no other experience to call on, I began to find events a little disarming.

We ventured a little further up the road, to where a gathering of Connor's fellow Irish workers had set up their own party. In the centre of their circle was a horizontal pig on a spit. It was golden and dripping hot fat as a man in a flat cap turned the handle. I watched the flickering shadows and inhaled the sensational aroma, imagining that every 'Pig Club' must have butchered a precious animal that day.

"Are you going to eat all that?" I asked, trying not to salivate and speculating over all the different cuts of meat.

"Oh, to be sure. Everything apart from the squeal," came the reply.

One of the navvies thrust a glass of what he told me was port into my hands. "That will put the roses back in yer cheeks," he announced. It was the first alcoholic drink I'd ever tried.

Taking a sip, I couldn't help pulling a face as it was too strong, too sharp, too everything for me. When some people nearby clambered on top of a car to dance, the roof collapsed, though nobody seemed bothered. It was wild and turning unruly, so I decided it was time to go home. I politely made an excuse, which probably wasn't audible over the din and slipped away, leaving them to their kerbside banquet.

Arriving back at the banjo in one piece, the first thing I noticed was that I hadn't been missed. Everyone was still carousing, but what had started off in the afternoon as a children's party and small bonfire had morphed into something more. People were raiding their Anderson shelters, pulling out the bunk beds and tossing them onto the fire, which had now doubled in size. I also spotted young men being sick in the bushes. Several children were standing around watching it all in their pyjamas, looking slightly distressed. I could only imagine they'd been put to bed before rejoining the party, unable to sleep. When I finally got my parents' attention and asked what time I should go to bed, they announced I could stay up as late as I wanted as there'd never be another night like this one. In the end, I actually took myself off to bed, happy and exhausted all at the same time. I'd heard so many conversations centred on the word 'tomorrow' that all the possibilities began chasing each other around in my head. London had taken it, but Valerie Braunston had also taken it, and she had come out the other side. I decided the sooner I got to sleep, the sooner tomorrow would come.

*

Our lives didn't come to a handbrake stop in May 1945, and nor was it some great starting gun for a new era. If anything, the immediate period after VE Day was something of a disappointment.

How could it be that, for me at least, the aftermath of the war was anticlimactic? You have to understand that for all my life I'd heard Pam saying, "before the war this" and "before the war that". Before the war you could get oranges and bananas; before the war cards were given away in tea and cigarette packets; before the war biscuits came in big tins filled to the brim, just there for the asking, and free toys came with boxes of cereal. But none of these appeared, and I also wondered what had happened to the sweets.

If anything, life was harder. Yes, the threat of imminent death had been lifted, but our war-torn country was on its knees and there was still fighting in the Pacific against the Japanese, which carried on until mid-August. It would be a long time before 'our boys' came home from those far-flung places and the prison camps.

Everything already rationed remained rationed, and then, after a bad harvest, my parents told me with forlorn looks that flour and bread were being added to the list. We now had another shortage. People grumbled. Hitler could no longer be the target of our wrath so who else could be to blame?

Everywhere I went, I saw unkept, unpainted buildings and dirty streets, and there were no road cleaners. Stepping outside to go and play at a friend's house meant crunching through broken glass and coming home with shoes coated with brick dust. Dad wanted to brighten up and paint our house, only to discover that with all the factories converted to producing camouflage colours, it might take months for any fresh, vibrant stock to come through. And so, unless you wanted your lounge to look like an army barracks, any immediate decorating was out of the question. Town halls and public buildings remained swaddled in the layers of sandbags that had been built higher each year of the war, as there wasn't the manpower to take them down. Bricked-up or ugly, bombed out houses needed to be tackled and rebuilt. It was difficult to know where to start.

The rebuilding effort came to the banjo when the playing fields by our house, which I'd known for most of the war years as the allotments, were designated for prefabricated homes. Within weeks, all we heard was crash-bang-wallop every day from the site as those new homes were swiftly erected. It was just temporary, they stated, like the allotments had been. My father never got the view back from his window. To my dismay, even the pond, Tinky Tonks, was filled in with brick rubble from the city. Apparently, it needed to go somewhere.

Dad wanted to know when the blast-damaged war memorials from the First World War would be repaired. I could tell it bothered him. Other families lobbied for new brass panels to accommodate the names of their sons who had more recently been lost. Some newspapers even started to talk about another war in the future with Russia, which only months ago had been an ally. It was as if some people couldn't get enough of fighting and destruction. We were all war weary. So maybe my description of being 'disappointed' was unfair. It just felt that even though we had nothing else to give, our sacrifices weren't yet over.

On top of all the housing and food issues, people like my dad needed work. The production of armaments had screeched to a halt and so huge numbers of men who'd enjoyed years of secure wages found themselves on the slagheap of unemployment. Stiff competition came from all the troops coming back after the war, their expectations high. Also spare a thought for a new band of disfigured and damaged men, all trying to find their way in this changed world.

My father desperately wanted to return to being an artist, although he remained sensible enough not to rush at it. He understood that it would take some time before people might treat themselves to the luxury of an oil painting. Mum never ceased to worry about paying the bills, but Dad remained a resourceful man, and having visited the shops he used to sell his artwork to, he declared over dinner that he would start the next day as a signwriter. There was a plethora of shopkeepers keen to reopen their doors and get back to business. He spent the first of many weeks atop a ladder, determined to carve out a living marking out and then painting new lettering over various shop fronts. Being outside in the fresh air and with a brush back in his hand, he looked much happier and brighter now. For years, I could walk along Main Avenue or visit the various corner shops of North London knowing that my dad had hand painted their signage.

Despite the general disruption brought by the war's conclusion, it was not all bad news for me. On the positive side, at least I wouldn't have to carry a gas mask ever again. The streetlights had also come back on, and I was introduced to the concept of 'evening', which hadn't existed for me in the winter war years. And then there was the simple pleasure of sleeping in my own bed knowing there would be no air raids or interruptions to contend with. My mother told me that every day during the war, when we all went our separate ways to school and to work, she would quietly pray that we would be together again come the evening. She was now spared that daily anxiety and could sleep deeply. In fact, without the shadow of war, we could all start to dream again.

Perhaps the most critical event for me that marked the end of the war and a return to normality was that I was expected to sit a school scholarship exam to determine where I should be headed next. What a topsy-turvy world. It only seemed like yesterday that I was in a village hall in Lincolnshire. I couldn't believe that after the schooling I'd received – or, more accurately, *not* received – that my near future would be mapped out by a short exam.

Initially, I didn't see the need for change, and I was quite content to remain where I was. I wanted my class to stay together, and no one explained to me that whether I passed the grammar school selection or not, we'd all inevitably have to go our separate ways. The thought of more disruption annoyed me, and, in my mind, failure was the best way of keeping my little gang together.

More exciting for me was that the Girl Guides would be re-starting. It was only something I'd heard about, and the waiting list was long, but I remained hopeful that I could get involved and maybe go on camps, like Pam had done "before the war". Yes, that phrase again!

I don't believe my parents left school with any qualifications, yet the end of the war made people think harder about what a bright new future could be. My dad couldn't be considered a progressive man, although he did tell me, "I'm glad I've got two girls, because they are more intelligent than boys. Now, don't go and ruin that!"

As the day of the exam neared, I recall my parents really beginning to encourage me. They knew I was easily distracted and so captured my interest with the opportunity to gain a reward. My classmate Beryl was going to get a new school bag if she passed, and Doreen talked about receiving a new fountain pen. Mum and Dad were happy to promise me an Enid Blyton Nature Lover's Diary if I passed, which was something I had coveted for ages. Such small incentives could sometimes work like magic.

On exam day, my mother took me to the large hall of the grammar school. As the desks around me rapidly filled up with all sorts of strange faces, it felt very daunting and competitive.

When silence fell, I waited for the command to open my test paper, now more determined to give a good account of myself.

Despite my previous reservations, I couldn't help but become totally engrossed in a composition, particularly as it afforded me the opportunity to have a good moan. There was a choice of five topics, and I selected the essay option entitled 'The Worst Day of My Life'. I let rip about being evacuated to Lincolnshire and being treated little better than the pigs. By contrast, the arithmetic paper was worse than I had expected. I completed what I could and then made wild guesses in the areas where I'd been flummoxed. The final paper was General Knowledge, and it consisted mostly of brief puzzles and substituting words. I found them so easy I suspected a catch.

To my utter astonishment, an official-looking letter arrived a few weeks later to say that I'd passed and would be required to attend Latymer School, a grammar school in Edmonton. To my relief, I soon discovered that some of my former classmates had also made the grade, and so I warmed to the idea.

I visited my old school one last time to say goodbye and thank you to my teachers. I impressed on them how I was going to work hard and either become an artist like my father, or an actress. They must have thought me terribly precocious.

Chapter 21
A Shiny Medal

I was in limbo over the summer break, as I waited with some trepidation to start my new school. Due to when my birthday fell, I would be one of the youngest in my year. Added to this, Latymer was also said to be the biggest school in the country. I just hoped I would be able to cope with what lay ahead.

With the exam now behind me and more things reopening, we started going out and doing more as a family. A big event was the circus coming to the recently built Harringay Arena. It starred Charlie Shadwell and his orchestra, which we'd heard many times on the radio but had never had the chance to see in the flesh. I was rather mesmerized by the showgirls who came out and paraded at the edge of the ring between each act, and I thought it might be a job to consider when I grew up. The fact that the girls were all at least six feet tall with legs up to their armpits never really struck me as a problem, as I still naively thought I would grow taller once the country had done with rationing. This was also the first time I'd seen clowns. Everyone kept nudging me in advance of them coming out to tell me how funny they were going to be, which, of course, was probably the worst thing to do. I couldn't understand why one of them kept tripping over his own feet, as it was something he was clearly doing on purpose. Having spent my childhood so far listening to clever wordplay and character comedy on the radio, I'd never seen visual jokes before.

With summer well and truly upon us, Dad kept his earlier promise that we should go on a family holiday. I was over the moon when he announced we would be visiting the Isle of Wight, which in my mind had been amplified to something of a mythical island, with sandy beaches hidden away off the coast. Apparently, Dad had managed to correspond with a bed and breakfast owner in Ventnor who was eager to reopen for trade.

We took a train south, and I remember the excitement of going on a steam ferry for the first time and tasting the salt in the air. It was then a further train journey across this green and pretty island to reach our destination. I'm not quite sure what I expected to find there, given the war had only recently ended, but I remember the shock of discovering that our accommodation was in an isolated spot set well-back on an inner cliff road. It also had no running water.

"Have they been bombed?" I asked in front of the landlady, as my parents whisked me behind them and closed ranks. I'd just assumed you wouldn't go on holiday to somewhere that didn't have taps! Every drop of water had to be manually pumped by hand, although the paying guests weren't expected to do the hard work, which might have been the last straw.

"Forget about the Girl Guides if you expect top-notch accommodation every time you go away," said my father. The family would have to make do yet again. At least we'd had lots of practice at that.

Pam and I shared a room, and in the morning, we found a bowl of cold water outside our door to wash with. In contrast, I recall my parents received a bowl of warm water for their use, because gentlemen were expected to shave.

There was one other guest staying at the same lodging, a lady of advancing years who was on her own. Her name was Miss Fletcher. She had been employed as a dresser at the Old Vic Theatre in London, and on that first evening, she delighted me with stories about working with actresses such as Valerie Hobson and Margaret Leighton. My interest was obvious, and these conversations only continued to fuel my ambitions.

On the other hand, Pam was less impressed by our bed and breakfast on a cliff with no other buildings in eyeshot. She had packed all her best clothes – it was a holiday, after all – but declared, hand on her hips, that "there was nobody to see," meaning there were no young men of her age here. I watched her remove three pairs of her best shoes from her case and line them up at the bottom of the wardrobe. One look at the farmer's fields at the back of the property suggested they weren't going to get any use.

On that first full morning, the sun was out, and I was keen to head to the beach. The landlady drew us a map and explained with much pointing how to get to the seafront at Ventnor. She also provided a large paper bag full of sandwiches for the day. Somehow, we took a wrong turn, which rendered the map useless, so we headed in the shortest direction to the coast, drawn by the distant sound of waves slapping onto rocks. That wasn't such a good idea. I was out in front and was the first to discover a line of cliffs and a sheer drop, guarded by reels of barbed wire stretching along the inner shoreline, still ready to impale or hold up the German hordes. Finding an opening in the wire, I then scrambled down, rock by rock, over crumbling banks and terraced steps, with everyone following in my trail.

"It was a damn site easier on the Western Front!" huffed Dad.

After discovering the beach, my parents approached the handful of other holidaymakers present, who told us this wasn't Ventnor at all, but a nearby place called Steephill Cove. However, it was rather stunning, and we decided that after such a trek, we would stay put.

When I opened the lunch bag, I discovered the sandwiches contained brawn (or jellied pig's head) and had unfortunately warmed somewhat over the course of the morning. I almost dry-retched. There was a debate as to who was going to politely decline the landlady's fare tomorrow without causing offence, and whether it would be better coming from an adult or a child. Pam, being something of an inbetweener, lost out and rolled her eyes. I couldn't be persuaded to remove the filling and still eat the bread, as the juices had seeped everywhere. It was going to be another hungry day for me. When no one was looking, I buried my sandwiches deep in the sand, suspecting that not even the crabs would fancy them.

Despite the lack of lunch, the slow pace and the delightful scenery worked its charm, and we all enjoyed the fine weather, the beach and looking out over the vastness of the English Channel. Often, we saw large ships sail by, presumably on their way to and from the great ports of Southampton or Portsmouth, and I played guessing games with Pam, stretching our imaginations as to what their precious cargos might be and when rationing would be lifted. It was only later that we learnt that the supplies of food were being shipped to Germany because the people there faced starvation.

That evening, the landlady told us about a local pub that had a 'children's room', which was a complete novelty for us, so we headed off down a country track to follow her recommendation. Fortunately, old habits die hard, and we each carried a torch with us, an essential item from the days of the blackouts that we hadn't yet learnt to give up. Each one still had tape stuck across half the reflector to push the beam downwards and comply with the old rules. In the end, after a splendid evening as a family, we spread ourselves across the country lane whilst singing a favourite music hall song. Dad, not usually much of a public performer, sang each verse of 'The Old Dun Cow', whilst the rest of us lustily joined in at every chorus:

"And there was Brown, upside down

Lickin' up the whiskey off the floor

"Booze! Booze!" the firemen cried

As they came knockin' at the door

Don't let them in till it's all mopped up

Somebody shouted "MacIntyre" (MacIntyre!)

And we all got blue blind

Paralytic drunk

When the Old Dun Cow caught fire"

*

On my first day at Latymer, my mum scraped my hair back so severely before plaiting it that I was afraid if a teacher had asked me a question, I wouldn't have been able to speak properly. As this was my first term, I had the bonus of a proper new uniform in navy and pale blue. Brand new clothes were still a novelty, and I stroked the fabric and stood in front of the mirror, adjusting the navy ribbons in my hair. I tried to ignore the fact that my parents had been economical by buying items at least a size too big for me.

That day, considering myself quite grown up, I travelled on the bus by myself. I had with me my shiny new satchel filled with sharpened pencils, ink pen, blotting paper and my Nature Lover's Diary, for good measure.

The school seemed enormous, particularly considering it wasn't long ago that I'd been taught in a one-room village school. Over one thousand pupils jostled through the corridors, and everywhere I looked, I saw an impossible number of noisy boys. We had two school halls; the oldest one was where we would be tucking in to our school dinners. Assemblies took place in a huge modern hall with a raised balcony, large enough that several year groups could come together. In our first assembly, I remember the headmaster making a solemn opening address and referencing the wooden shields over the entrance, freshly inscribed in gold lettering with the names of the 'old boys' who had died in the war. It set a serious tone for the day ahead. After that, the headmaster quickly disappeared and must have busied himself elsewhere. In my mind, he was a distant figure who never contributed anything valuable to school life. All the previous heads I'd known had also taken us for lessons.

Discipline was the responsibility of various senior masters and mistresses, and these people would rule our lives. My year group was split into six classes and my form tutor was Mr Chapman, who taught maths. That didn't bode too well for me! Maths now had the devilish added complications of algebra and geometry. Mr Chapman had a cutting sense of humour, which mostly fell on deaf ears. He was not averse to hurling chalk or the blackboard rubber at his pupils, usually the boys. I quickly felt sorry for the males in my class, because they all got addressed by their surnames and the teachers would often take a harder line with them. It took me a long time to work out everyone's Christian names. Whilst I didn't need to duck from flying chalk, I was on the receiving end of Mr Chapman's acerbic wit. I remember him reading out the results of a test one day following my lacklustre attempt at revision. "Valerie Braunston – a nice round figure," he announced. It was some time before I realised I'd received a 'o'.

Science, which had previously been heavily biased to biology, was now broken up into its three constituent parts. Although I still largely enjoyed biology, the sight of my teacher waving around a sheep's lungs like a yachtsman trying to catch the wind was off-putting. Nor did I particularly want to dissect a rat that had done me no harm. Subjects such as chemistry and physics (which to my mind were just another form of maths) were bamboozling. English, my best academic subject, had been split into English grammar and English literature. Gone were the days when I could write my whimsical compositions (which at the time I'd thought were great works), as I realised they wouldn't cut the mustard at Latymer. On that first day, I kept asking myself how I'd managed to get into this school, and I wondered if I would be able to keep up.

We also started to learn German as our foreign language, which would be useful if we were ever invaded. I studied our teacher with suspicion for the first few lessons before accepting that he was a certified Englishman. After that, I got into the rhythm of things and became reasonably proficient. Once we had an ear for the accent, it was also the source of endless Hitler impersonations and tomfoolery in the playground.

Looking back now, I realise that once again, we were rather short changed when it came to teachers. Ours had generally lost their spark and many were quick to point out that class sizes were higher than in pre-war times. We also suffered from a shortage of the basic things like textbooks, which hadn't been replenished in years. In turn, we often had to share one between three, which meant that even in this elevated status of a grammar school, any homework set for a week's time needed to be completed within two days, as I was expected to pass the book on to the next person, and so on.

My first school report was nothing to write home about and it rattled around in my satchel for several days, getting crumpled. When I finally handed it over to my parents for their signature, to my relief they were quite sanguine about it. Perhaps just me being at a grammar school was sufficient for them.

Salvation came when we were allowed to pick one subject of our choice. Without any hesitation, I chose drama. That's where I met Reverend E J Burton, who probably had the greatest influence over my post-school life than any other teacher. Reverend Burton was a clever, handsome man, who was possibly in his mid-thirties. He was first introduced to us as our divinity master. It was clear from the outset that he was quite different to the stuffy types that I'd previously been taught by. Indeed, he came across as a little bit potty and was quite a favourite with the girls.

From the moment he took me for drama, it was a mind-boggling experience. One of his famous techniques was known as SPONS (or spontaneous dramatics), which today would be called improvisation. It was a rare thing back in an age where tradition and conformity were the expectation. This was austere post-war Britain, not the swinging 60s. To suddenly have a drama teacher challenging us to become a character, or an inanimate object, or to work without a script, was like being taken to a different world for a few minutes. Soon, acting was all I thought about, and for me, it was the only thing that made going to school worthwhile.

I revelled in this environment, although it wasn't to everyone's taste. At first, it seemed as if the whole year group had chosen the subject, as many considered it to be the soft option. But the numbers were quickly whittled down to what became an enthusiastic and, some might say, elite group of students. At this point, I loved drama even more. Expectations were set high, and we were made aware of the alumni, which included Maurice Meredith, who went on to teach maths on early TV broadcasts, as well as Valerie Walsh, a well-known dancer of her day. I was happy to try and rise to the challenge.

At this point, I was first selected to represent my house against another pupil in my year group called Eileen Atkins (who later became Dame Eileen Atkins, a BAFTA Television Award, Emmy, and three-time Olivier Award-winning actress). We vied for first and second place on a number of occasions, and I could often be found walking home from the bus stop enthusiastically practising my poem or drama piece at the top of my voice, attracting odd stares from the people around me.

It became apparent that Eileen had a very special quality about her. The Reverend Burton had singled her out for extra tuition, but I wasn't jealous – I simply admired her talent and was inspired to try even harder. At school, in a production of Shakespeare's King John, she was the young Prince Albert, and as she pleaded not to be blinded with a red-hot branding iron – "Will you put out mine eyes?" – I got goosebumps. I didn't see the young girl or the school uniform, I only saw a youth pleading for her sight.

Lobbying Reverend Burton, I suggested that one day I could be an actress and would put in whatever hard work was required to improve my skills. With kind words, he told me that it might take years for me to reach my goal. He pointed out that Eileen was like one of my father's blank canvases and could take on any part he asked her to play. In contrast, he believed I was 'the little dark one' and 'the spirited one' and might be a character actress but not the lead. I'm not sure I took all his advice in at the time. All I knew was that I was regularly on stage giving it my all, and sometimes winning minor spoken English or school competitions. My room at home had a growing collection of certificates and rosettes that I was very proud of. I continued to tell everyone I was going to be an actress one day. Oh, how I cringe now at my conceit.

Our school also had a reputation for verse speaking, and every year we would enter some quite prestigious competitions. On the basis that Eileen and I had tied in our most recent school competition, the Reverend Burton asked us both to work together on a duologue he had selected. We were to perform it in an inter-school competition covering the whole of North

London. I remember Mum lending me a very precious pair of silk stockings for the event.

The piece the Reverend had selected for us was a simple verse told by Eileen and me, representing two nuns. As we sat in the theatre watching the other competitors take their turn, my heart sank because their pieces were from well-known plays and were quite sophisticated compared to our skit. I didn't think we stood a chance. I knew Eileen also shared my misgivings. So, imagine our surprise when we were announced as the winners. Our duologue piece turned out to be a rather clever choice by our teacher because it was both charming and suited our young ages.

For the first and only time in my life, I received a medal. Not a certificate or a rosette – a shiny medal! My dad had medals with his name on them and now I had one of my own. This was going to take pride of place in my bedroom. My good old lucky penny, already relegated to a drawer in my room, was thin and dull by comparison.

I was happy with my life, happier than I could ever remember being. If you could have seen Eileen and me, we were not very nun-like as we dashed off the bus on the main road near school, desperate to locate the Reverend Burton and share our success. We both ran back to school around the edge of the school fields, my mouth full of gobstoppers and Eileen doing cartwheels. As I kicked through the tall, uncut grass, I sent a pair of Holly Blue butterflies tumbling upwards into the sky, and for a few moments, it was as if they were racing with me. Two little blue specks danced around me, intrepid and wilful, before my courageous little wanderers darted away to safety.

My medal glinted in the sunshine. As we reached the main building, a small but enthusiastic crowd surrounded us, as if drawn to our energy. I held my prize aloft, wanting everyone to see my achievement. For the first time in my life, it felt like the war was truly behind me and just about anything was possible.

Afterword

Valerie Braunston continued to correspond with Miss Talbot until the 1950s. After attending Latymer Grammar, she achieved a huge ambition by being accepted into the Royal Academy of Dramatic Art (RADA). However, to her lifelong frustration, she only attended for one term as she wasn't able to gain the scholarship required to make the fees affordable for her parents. Valerie was active in amateur dramatics, where she met her future husband, Jack Bingham. They married in 1959, and for several decades, they both acted in and produced many productions, first in Enfield and then later in Brighton and Hove. After becoming a mother, Valerie took up art again in the 1970s and became a successful watercolour artist, selling over 1,000 paintings to help support her family. For over a decade, she sold her work alongside her father. As a tribute to him, she always painted in her maiden name.

During the 1990s and 2000s, Valerie became active on the after-dinner speaking circuit, delivering many talks to members' clubs such as the Women's Institute on a variety of subjects, including her wartime memories.

At the age of 80, she had her first book published. Called The Rocky Road to La La Land, it chronicled life with her husband both before and after he was diagnosed with dementia. Recently, at the age of 88, Valerie went into a care home suffering from dementia herself. She passed away only months later.

Valerie was always intrigued by what might have been her Jewish ancestry on her father's side, but she never got to the truth. As far as she knew, her father had been christened at birth in London, as both she and Pam were. Then, around the time she went into care, her family was contacted by a genealogist from Australia who had been researching recently made available records through the Israel Genealogy Society. These revealed the active role of the 19th-century Anglican Christ Church in Jerusalem in converting Jewish people to the Anglican faith and included specific references to Valerie's grandfather (see Philipe Braunstein).

Horace 'Len' Braunstein was a young man at the outbreak of the First World War and, like so many of his generation, he raced to join up. At the time, he was just 17 years old, so he lied about his age. At the point of attesting, he was advised by the recruiters to change his surname, which is how he became a Braunston. He joined the 2nd Battalion of the Queen Victoria Rifles (9th London Regiment). In the early years of the war, his battalion remained in the UK, where they underwent training before moving into civil defence. With casualties mounting at the Western Front, the 2nd Battalion was shipped to France in March 1917 and transported to the trenches in Belgium. During the 1917 battle of Passchendaele, Horace went 'over the top' in a large-scale attack where his battalion suffered a 50%

casualty rate. The battlefield trench map he brought back from that engagement includes his scribbled notes and is still in the family. A copy also resides in the Passchendaele 1917 Museum in Flanders.

At some point in early 1918, Horace became a casualty of mustard gas. He was rescued from the battlefield by his best friend, Frank, who by chance happened to be deployed from another battalion as a stretcher bearer that day. Due to the effects of gas inhalation, Horace was evacuated back to the UK for convalescence and was deemed no longer fit for active service.

He married Irene Bickmore in 1926 and was a successful artist all his life, supporting his wife and two children by selling his oil paintings. After the Second World War, the couple opened a shop/studio in Enfield where Horace painted, and Irene sold china and small collectibles. In the 1960s, the family moved from North London down to Hove for the sea air. Although Irene died of cancer in 1976, Horace continued to paint and sell his art up to the point of his death in 1983. He was found dead aged 85, after collapsing on the floor of his studio with a half-finished canvas on his easel. He had outlived eight siblings.

Due to the mustard gas, he coughed badly all his life. He would rarely be drawn on his service in the First World War and was never known to wear a poppy or join any regimental reunions. However, he always kept his box of souvenirs.

Pam Braunston was born in Ilford in 1926. Following the war, she developed her career in retail fashion and cosmetics, moving on to become an international buyer before marrying in 1949. Sadly, her first husband died only two years later of a heart attack. Not long after, she remarried a British military officer, and they spent many years living abroad, where he was posted to several countries, including Egypt, Cyprus and Kenya. They finally settled in Southport, where they brought up two children. Pam died in 1978.

Horace's father was Philipe Braunstein (1849-1930). Available records show that in the mid-1860s, when he was 16, he entered Jerusalem from Russia with his parents. They stayed at a poor house run by the Anglican Church, where the whole family was given lodgings and a trade to learn in exchange for agreeing to be converted and baptised. At the age of 20, Philipe emigrated from Jerusalem and travelled to London, eventually building a successful rubber stamp and ink business.

Valerie's surviving Grannie and Grandpa during the war period were Ellen Hardy (1873-1946) and Robert Bickmore (1871-1964). Grannie Ellen died in Ilford aged 73, whilst Grandpa Robert lived to the grand age of 94. He died after being hit by a bus crossing the road in Ilford to post his pools coupon.

Phil Braunstein was one of Horace's older brothers, and he also joined up in 1914, serving with the 1st Essex Heavy Battery as an artilleryman. Military records show that he was classed as 'Illegally Absent' from his unit in the spring of 1915, whilst they were stationed in Suffolk. Having absconded, Phil next reappeared in Calgary, Canada, where the passenger shipping records reveal he made the crossing using the name Brownston. Within weeks of arriving in Calgary, he joined the Canadian Army as an artilleryman (still under the name Brownston) and later served with the Canadian forces on the Western Front.

After the war, he returned to Canada and made a life there. Due to being classed as AWOL from the British Army, he was unable or unwilling to visit the UK until 1959.

Further Information

Gas Masks

Britain entered the Second World War in September 1939, just twenty years after the end of the First World War. Given that the previous war had included the mass use of poison gas by all sides, every adult, child and baby was issued a gas mask at the outbreak of this new conflict.

Evacuations

The mass evacuation of children also began at the outbreak of war. In just a few days, approximately 1.5 million people, including over 800,000 children, were relocated from major cities during the government-planned Operation Pied Piper, which is believed to be the largest orchestrated movement of people up to that point. Further waves of evacuations (and re-evacuations) followed, displacing an estimated three million people.

When the war first broke out, there was a lengthy period known as the 'phoney war' – a time when, apart from blackouts and the introduction of rationing, the country wasn't under direct attack. Having not felt welcome in their rural surroundings, many of the evacuees who had fled to the countryside returned during this period.

Towards the end of the war, during the V-1 rocket campaign, another mass exodus took place. Again, an estimated 1.5 million people fled London, though this time only about 20% were 'official' evacuees.

Dig for Victory

At the start of the war, a large percentage of Britain's food was imported, a significant vulnerability that had already been exposed by the Germans in World War One. The 'Dig for Victory' campaign began as soon as war broke out, with many public parks and green spaces converted for food production. By 1945, Britain had an estimated 1.4 million allotments, and 70% of food was being produced locally.

Pets in WWII

At the start of the war, the government launched a campaign encouraging people to have their pets put down, in preparation for the worst. Records show that approximately 750,000 pets were euthanised due to the campaign's success, while many others were likely abandoned by their owners.

Rationing

Rationing began at the outbreak of the war, covering most food commodities, and restrictions became increasingly tight as the war progressed. In addition to food, clothes (and cloth), petrol and coal were also rationed. Laws were relaxed to allow urban communities to form 'Pig Clubs' to supplement meagre rations.

These groups looked after one or more pigs themselves, using scraps for feed. Officially, half of a slaughtered pig was to be handed over to the Ministry of Food, while the remainder could be shared among club members. Many thousands of Pig Clubs were established by groups of workers.

Interestingly, many items continued to be rationed after the war, with some additional rationing measures introduced. For example, as Valerie mentions in her memoir, bread and flour were rationed for the first time in 1946 after a poor harvest, and this continued until 1948. In 1947, potato rationing was introduced due to further bad weather. Clothes were rationed until 1949 and petrol until 1950. The 1950 General Election was fought largely on the issue of rationing and when it might end. That year, petrol rationing ceased, but it wasn't until 1953 that sweets, sugar and confectionery were no longer rationed. In 1954, nearly nine years after the war had ended, meat rationing also came to an end. Finally, in 1958, coal rationing was lifted.

The Blitz

Following the Allied defeat in continental Europe and the evacuation at Dunkirk, Hitler sought air superiority over Britain to protect his invading army. When the Luftwaffe failed to dominate British skies, they turned to strategic bombing of British infrastructure and cities. After exploratory raids on city targets, docks and airfields, the Germans launched Operation Loge on 7 September 1940, targeting London (with 'Loge' as the codename for the city), which the British press called 'the Blitz' (derived from blitzkrieg). Initially, the raids were conducted during the day in an effort to draw British fighter planes into battle for destruction. Soon, however, the focus shifted to nighttime raids. The terror lasted eight months, ending on 10 May 1941, and included 57 consecutive nights of bombings in London.

At the time, London was the largest city in the developed world and the administrative centre of a vast empire, making it a practical and symbolic target. If the bombings proved overwhelming and the population rose in protest, the British government might be forced to capitulate.

It is likely that London withstood the Blitz because of its large size, which allowed it to absorb the raids. Greater London spans over 600 square miles, so concentration of bombing force – still a developing tactic – was hard to achieve. Consequently, other major cities were targeted in late October, though these raids were primarily harassing or diversionary. From November onward, the focus shifted again, and other cities experienced major raids. Coventry was partially destroyed in what was arguably the most devastating single raid of the war, whilst Liverpool became a key target due to its role as a major port and transport link with America.

London remained the primary target, not only because it was the capital but also due to the limited range of German fighter escorts. Possibly the most destructive air raid on London occurred on 29–30 December, when incendiary bombs ignited a firestorm that devastated a larger area than the Great Fire of London. Statistically, London experienced 71 'major' raids (defined as raids dropping at least 100 tons of bombs), while Liverpool and Birmingham each suffered eight. Some large cities were bombed relatively lightly, including Nottingham (one major raid), Sheffield (two), Belfast (two) and Cardiff (two).

By the end of the Blitz, an estimated 43,000 people had died, more than half of them in London. Additionally, approximately two million homes were badly damaged, 60% of which were in the capital. (Source: *The Night Blitz 1940-1941,* John Ray, 2006.)

Landmine Bombs

Landmine bombs were a wartime innovation arising from the Blitz. Originally developed as sea mines to attack metal Allied ships, they became obsolete once the British learned to neutralise the magnetic fields around Royal Navy ships. With a large stockpile left unused, the Germans adapted these weapons for use in the Blitz. These landmines (also known as parachute bombs) were dropped by bombers attached to parachutes and designed to detonate at rooftop height using a timed fuse. This setup allowed the shockwaves to travel unimpeded over a much wider distance than standard high-explosive bombs, which typically penetrated the ground before detonating. A large 1-tonne bomb, nicknamed 'Hefty Hermann' or 'Hermann Bomb' by both the British and Germans, was named after the portly German military leader Hermann Göring. During excavation work for the 2012 London Olympics, a 1-tonne bomb was discovered on Three Mills Island. It was the largest WWII bomb unearthed in decades and required five days to safely disarm.

ARP (Air Raid Precautions)

At the outbreak of war, Air Raid Precaution (ARP) wardens were organised by each local council to enforce blackouts, guide people to shelters and report bombings. They formed part of a vast volunteer Civil Defence Service, which, along with messengers, ambulance drivers, observers, first-aiders and fire guards, enabled London and other major cities to function during and after raids. Approximately 1.9 million people volunteered for Civil Defence, with an increasing proportion of women. However, images of Londoners sheltering in the underground and on station platforms give a misleading impression of shelter availability at the time. Only an estimated 4% of the population used underground stations, and 9% used official large-scale shelters. Most Londoners stayed at home, enduring the bombing in improvised shelters.

London Can Take It!

London Can Take It! was a British propaganda film created in 1940 to depict the impact of eighteen hours of German bombing on London and its people. The film's main audience was American citizens, with the goal of garnering sympathy for Britain's plight. At the time, many Americans viewed Britain as a fading imperial power. This film was part of a broader campaign to encourage the then-neutral United States to join the fight against Germany. Joseph Goebbels, quoted in the film, claimed that the bombings were significantly affecting British morale. "He is right," the narrator responds, "the British people's morale is now higher than ever!" Produced by the British Ministry of Information, the film has become an iconic piece of wartime media, embodying the resilient 'Blitz spirit' that characterised working-class London. In the US, it was released as London Can Take It!, while a shorter domestic version was titled Britain Can Take It, likely to avoid appearing London-centric and alienating other UK cities also enduring bombings.

Antisemitism

Antisemitism was widespread in the UK throughout the early 1900s, appearing in many influential novels of the time, including works by Agatha Christie. In the 1930s, such sentiments intensified with the rise of fascist and nationalist movements across Europe. During the Blitz, as Jewish residents were evacuated from London's East End (where many had lived before the war), reports indicated a growing wave of antisemitism in rural areas receiving Jewish evacuees. Another instance of antisemitism followed the Bethnal Green Tube Disaster in 1943, when a crowd crush on the station stairs killed 173 people. Rumours spread that the tragedy had been caused by a stampede of Jewish people seeking safety. Records of these events were classified as sensitive and archived by the National Archive, only becoming public in 2018.

Pea-Souper

The term 'smog' combines 'smoke' and 'fog' and describes a thick, often yellow or greenish industrial pollution that plagued large cities at the time. Another term for this dense smog was 'pea-souper'. In London, it was believed that airborne dust from bombed buildings worsened the smog. It was a frequent winter phenomenon until the Great Smog of 1952, which ultimately led to the Clean Air Act of 1956.

The Baby Blitz

The 'Baby Blitz' began in January 1944 and ended in May of that year. Frustrated by constant Allied bombings, Hitler ordered retaliatory raids focused on Central London and Southern

England, although other regions were occasionally targeted. With only around 500 bombers available, the Luftwaffe relied on increasingly obsolete planes with inexperienced crews, as resources had shifted towards fighter production for Germany's defence. About 70% of the German aircraft were lost during the campaign. By this time, Britain's defences included squadrons of Mosquito night fighters and nearly 3,000 anti-aircraft guns in London alone. Despite this, a further 1,556 British civilians were killed in the Baby Blitz.

The V-1 Rocket

The first V-1 rocket, also known as the 'doodlebug' or 'buzzbomb,' launched on 13th June 1944, hitting Grove Road and destroying a railway bridge and nearby homes, killing six people. A second V-1 landed farther afield, striking Epping. London was the primary target, with all rockets aimed at Tower Bridge. Initially, Britain had little defence against this new weapon. Over the following months, approximately 10,000 V-1s were launched at Southern England, reaching a peak of 100 launches per day. By August, British countermeasures improved, intercepting about 80% of launched missiles. As the Allies advanced into Europe post-D-Day, they overran many V-1 launch sites, which were then relocated inland. Nearly 2,500 V-1 rockets successfully struck Greater London, killing over 6,000 people. Nine out of 10 UK fatalities from V-1s occurred in London.

Enfield Small Arms

The renowned Enfield Small Arms factory near the River Lea first opened in 1816, benefiting from the river's water power and a direct link to the Lee Navigation system for transport. Known for producing the Lee-Enfield rifle and other firearms during both world wars, it employed thousands at its peak. The factory closed in 1963, and in 1990, a nightclub named 'Rifles' opened on the redeveloped site.

Italian Prisoners of War

After mounting defeats in North Africa and the Middle East in 1941, large numbers of Italian prisoners of war (PoWs) were sent to the UK, where they helped alleviate labour shortages, particularly in agriculture, in line with the Geneva Convention. Initially housed in internment camps, PoWs were later dispersed across rural areas as needed. Prisoners wore armbands denoting their fascist sympathies and flight risk. Following Italy's surrender in 1943, 100,000 Italians volunteered as 'co-operators' to work under less restrictive conditions. By war's end, 400,000 Italians were in the UK, and many stayed on to aid post-war reconstruction.

The V-2 Rocket

The V-2, the world's first ballistic missile, was developed by Nazi Germany and instilled fear because it struck without warning. The V-2 offensive began in September 1944 and continued until March 1945, with 97% of rockets targeting London. Although many V-2s missed their targets, over 1,200 hit London, killing nearly 3,000 people. The only effective defence against the V-2 involved locating and destroying its launch sites.

Bush Hill Park

Bush Hill Park, in the borough of Enfield, recorded a total of 571 high-explosive bombs and seven parachute bombs during the Blitz. Later, the area was struck by 41 V-1 and 26 V-2 rockets.

The V-3 Rocket

A V-3 'terror weapon' was also secretly developed, though it was never used. Known as the 'London Cannon,' this fixed-position long-range gun was designed to bombard the capital with large shells, but construction was incomplete.